The Streets of Hampstead

Christopher Wade

© Camden History Society 2000

ISBN 0 904491 46 3

The Streets of Hampstead

Third edition, newly revised by   Christopher Wade

Edited by   F Peter Woodford

Designed by   Ivor Kamlish

*Portion of Rocque's map of
London, published 1746*

First published 1972   *Second edition* 1984

Diagrammatic map of the walks

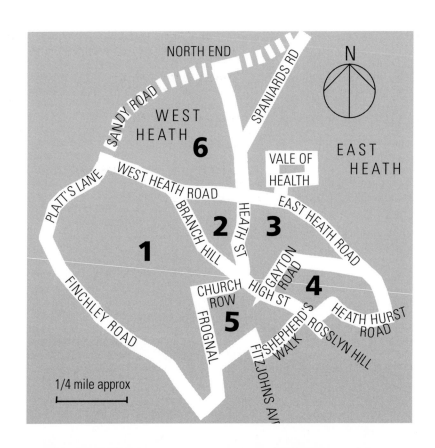

NORTH END

SPANIARDS RD

N

SANDY ROAD

WEST
HEATH **6**

VALE OF
HEALTH

EAST
HEATH

PLATT'S LANE

WEST HEATH ROAD

EAST HEATH ROAD

BRANCH HILL

HEATH ST

2 **3**

1

GAYTON ROAD

4

CHURCH ROW

HIGH ST

5

HEATH HURST ROAD

FINCHLEY ROAD

FROGNAL

SHEPHERD'S WALK

ROSSLYN HILL

FITZJOHNS AV.

1/4 mile approx

Contents

Acknowledgements

Much of the research for the first edition of this book was done by CHS members: Shirley Harris, Brenda Tyler, Diana Wade, and Wilfred Meadows, who led the group. Other helpful informants have included David Hellings, Christopher Ikin, John Price, David Sullivan, Wendy Trewin and Philip Venning.

The columns of the *Hampstead & Highgate Express* have been most useful, as have Malcolm Holmes, Richard Knight and the staff of Camden's Local Studies and Archives Centre (CLSAC).

The following sources of illustration are gratefully acknowledged: CLSAC, John Richardson (*Historical Publications*), Ken Pyne, and the Hampstead Museum at Burgh House, Hampstead.

A note on typeface codes

Buildings named or numbered in the text in bold type were extant and visible at the time of writing (October 1999); those in roman type had either been demolished or had otherwise faded into the past.

Abbreviations

CHR	*Camden History Review*
CHS	Camden History Society
DCMS	Department for Culture, Media and Sport
DNB	*Dictionary of National Biography*
DOE	Department of the Environment
GLC	Greater London Council
Ham&High	*Hampstead and Highgate Express*
ICI	Imperial Chemical Industries
LCC	London County Council
O.S.	Ordnance Survey
RIBA	Royal Institute of British Architects
Tate	Tate Gallery, Millbank
TUC	Trades Union Council
UCS	University College School
V&A	Victoria and Albert Museum

Illustrations

Introduction

The essential equipment for a local historian, said that great authority A L Rowse, is a strong pair of boots. Libraries and record offices can provide plentiful topographical detail about a locality, but the only way of checking the facts is by walking the streets.

This book began as a project launched by the Camden History Society in 1970 to discover the origins of Camden's street names. So much research was involved, digging into Rate Books, Manor Minutes, Street Directories and Camden's own Local History Collection, that the Hampstead group soon found that they had a mass of splendid information not only about streets but also about houses and residents. And so, in 1972, appeared the Society's first walk-about historical guide for the Man and Woman in the Street, the first edition of this book. It was much helped by being published by the High Hill Press. Six more Camden street surveys in this style have been published since then (see back cover), and the series will eventually embrace all the streets of the Borough.

The area covered by this book, usually called Old Hampstead (preferably not 'the village'), is rich in remarkable architecture, ancient and modern, and notable for its flocks of famous residents. As an earlier historian cried, after a spate of name-dropping, 'Where shall the brilliant roll conclude?'

The dates and details of historic buildings have been taken largely from the latest Lists compiled by the DCMS (see note below on Listed Buildings). Much information and colourful comment has come from Sir Nikolaus Pevsner's Buildings of England series, including a recently published volume on North London, with Bridget Cherry as co-author. Some comments from Sir Nikolaus' first, 1952, edition have been quoted, always in the past tense.

With respect to the eminent residents, the main interest in this survey has been to find out why they came to Hampstead and what they did while they were here, as well as what effect they had on the neighbourhood and vice versa. The many celebrities currently resident in the area have not been included, for the sake of their peace and privacy.

As before, it has to be stressed that this book offers what can only be a personal selection from the mountains of material available. Readers are warmly encouraged to report additional findings about Hampstead's intriguing history. But Stendhal's awful warning about historical exploration remains true: "It is terrifying to think how much research is needed to determine the truth of even the most unimportant fact."

Christopher Wade
Hampstead, October 1999

A note on plaques

Hampstead has more plaques than any other London suburb. Blue Plaques predominate, and these are 'official' in that they are organised and controlled by English Heritage. Candidates for these plaques must either be dead for 20 years or born 100 years ago. They must also have 'a strong reputation and have gained recognition through their life and work'. Official ceramic plaques were first erected by the Royal Society of Arts in 1867 and they were brown. Round blue plaques began in 1901, when the LCC took over the scheme. English Heritage has been in charge since 1986. Black plaques, oval and metallic, have been erected by the Hampstead Plaque Fund (originated by Ralph Wade), applying no particular rules. They are now supervised by the Heath and Hampstead Society. Private plaques of various shapes and styles have been erected – and anyone can do so on any house, as long as the owner (and perhaps the Planning Department of the Local Authority) agrees.

Listed buildings

Hampstead has many 'Buildings of Special Architectural or Historic Interest', which are officially listed by a Government Department. The 1974 List was issued by the Department of the Environment (DOE). A revised List was published in 1998 by the Department for Culture, Media and Sport (DCMS). A copy of the List may be consulted at the Planning Department in Camden Town Hall. The topmost, exceptional, grade used in the Lists is I, followed by the fairly rare II*, and finally II. Grades sometimes relate to the interiors of houses rather than the building as a whole.

Hampstead's Grade I buildings are the Parish Church, St John's Downshire Hill, St Stephen's Rosslyn Hill, Burgh House, Fenton House, Keats House, Romney's House and the house (No.6 Ellerdale Road) which Norman Shaw built and lived in himself. Most of the houses in Church Row are graded II*, while most of the houses in Downshire Hill are grade II.

From the Ham&High, 16 Oct 98

9

Historical overview

The name Hampstead comes from the Old English *Hamestede*, meaning homestead or manor. There are Hampsteads – and variations like Hemel Hempstead – all over the country and in the old colonies. The Hampstead in New Hampshire (USA) was founded in 1749 and named 'in honour of the pleasant village in Middlesex County'.

The documentary history of the manor dates back to the charter of AD 986, in which King Ethelred (the Unready) gave the land to the monks of Westminster. The original charter (there is a copy in the British Museum) was almost certainly a forgery, but probably recorded an oral tradition for the gift and was necessary to establish the Abbey's title to the manor. According to this and other Anglo-Saxon charters, the boundaries of Hampstead were practically the same in the 10th century as they were nearly 1000 years later, when the borough was absorbed by Camden – from North End down to Primrose Hill, and from the Heath across to Kilburn High Road – approximately 2000 acres.

The manor was valued at only 50 shillings in the Domesday Book of 1086, and the picture it gives is of a small farm with fodder for 100 pigs in a clearing of the vast Middlesex Forest. The farm furnished the monks of Westminster with fresh produce throughout the Middle Ages, but the only recorded visit of importance by the monks was during the Black Death. Abbot Simon de Barcheston fled to Hampstead for his health, but he brought the plague with him and died here in 1349.

After Henry VIII's dissolution of the monasteries, the manor passed into lay hands, beginning in 1551 with Sir Thomas Wroth, a favourite of Edward VI. The first of Hampstead's absentee landlords, Wroth sold the property in 1620 to Baptist Hickes, later Lord Campden (not to be confused with Camden), the mercer and moneylender, who also owned land in the Notting Hill area and around Chipping Campden. Noted for their good works, his family in 1643 founded a charity for the poor of Hampstead. So did the Earl of Gainsborough's family, who inherited the manor; they donated some land around Well Walk in 1698. Their gifts are now united in the Wells and Campden Charity, which today has assets of some £12 million.

To complete the manor's history, it was sold to Sir William Langhorne in 1707 and later passed by marriage to the Maryon, later Maryon Wilson, family. It was Sir Thomas Maryon Wilson who fought to the death to build houses on the Heath; his fight ended only when he died in 1869. The Heath was bought for the public 2 years later. Though the manor as such is now defunct, a great-great-nephew of Sir Thomas still owns a slice of Hampstead.

From village to suburb

Much of Hampstead's history is connected with its hill, its heath and its healthy air and water. There is a layer of Bagshot sand on the crest of the hill, a sand much prized and excavated over the centuries by the builders of London. The sand explains both the heath, once more scrubby and gorsey than it is now, and the water supplies. The rain percolates through the sand until it meets the top layer of clay, and then emerges as springs and streams, including three rivers – the Tyburn, the Westbourne and the Fleet. The first two are more or less 'lost rivers', but some of the early Fleet can be seen flowing on the Heath and filling the ponds. Hampstead was long famous for its pure water, and a colony of laundresses was established here by the 16th century. It was said that rivermen on the Thames would look up at Hampstead and think it snow-capped, but it was really the linen left out to dry.

At the end of the 17th century, reports of the chalybeate (or ferruginous) well near Well Walk turned Hampstead into a spa known as Hampstead Wells. The fact that the water had such a peculiarly nasty taste must have contributed to its medicinal value, which was probably as real as the maladies of many who drank it. Though the popularity of the Spa depended chiefly on day-trippers from London, boarding houses and villas were built for temporary residents and, when the popularity of the Wells died, about the same time that Queen Anne did (1714), these houses were developed into permanent residences. By then, Hampstead had become known as a health resort, and this was responsible for most of the fine new buildings of the 18th century.

After a second Spa period later in the century Hampstead was, according to its first historian J J Park, 'the permanent residence of a select, amicable, respectable and opulent neighbourhood'. But in 1815, the year after Park's book was published, a visitor noted 'hundreds of mean houses and alleys'. Hampstead had grown too fast for general comfort. Another visitor in the 1870s remarked on 'Hampstead's narrow and dirty by-ways . . . and mean and crowded tenements'. Fortunately, many of these were swept away by the Town Improvements scheme of the 1880s, which changed the face of upper High Street and lower Heath Street.

By then, the gap had been closed between Hampstead and the spreading city. In 1888 the town ceased to be in the Parish of St John, Hampstead, Middlesex, and officially became part of London. The first Hampstead Borough Council was formed in 1900, under the aegis of the London County Council, and was taken over by Camden Council in 1965. Hampstead has now lost its autonomy, but is not without a mind of its own.

Street history

The discovery of some Roman pottery in Well Walk in 1774 supported the old theory that there was a Roman road across Hampstead Heath, but no firm evidence has been found. If the Romans used a route through central Hampstead as an alternative to Watling Street when that low-lying track became waterlogged, it is probable that they used the main thoroughfare that exists today. Once a High Street, always a High Street.

Nearly all the routes on Rocque's map of 1746 (opposite title-page) have survived to this day, though many have changed in importance. For instance, Rocque suggests that Holly Hill, rather than Heath Street, was the main link between High Street and Whitestone Pond, but this was reversed by the early 19th century. Many early tracks led to wells and windmills, and the popularity of Holly Hill may have derived from the two mills near its summit.

The first accurate map of Hampstead's streets was the Ordnance Survey of 1866, but this was before the development of the lower stretches of Frognal and Heath Street and of the Gayton, Willoughby and Redington Road areas.

The naming of streets was always a haphazard affair and, before the Penny Post of 1840, few of them had official titles. Names of landowners and pubs predominated, but the Victorians changed many of them to improve their image or because they preferred purely fanciful names. It also seems that builders gave their roads pretty names to attract customers who would pay pretty prices.

Route 1
The Manor
From Frognal to West Heath Road

Start at the lower end of Frognal, at the junction with Finchley Road.

There never was a Manor House in Hampstead nor, for that matter, a resident Lord of the Manor. But up until the 19th century there was a scatter of buildings at the junction of Frognal and Frognal Lane (formerly West End Lane, see Fig 1) which belonged to the Lord and, in particular, to his Manor Farm,

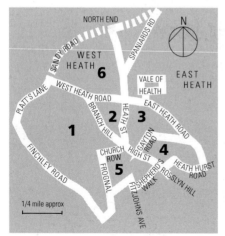

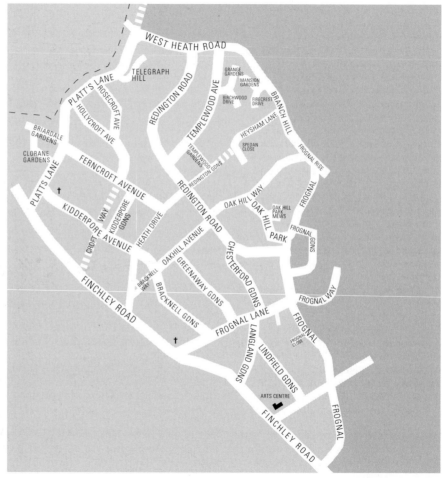

also known as Hall Oak Farm.
Hereabouts was the earliest settlement
of the hamlet of Hampstead, an
agricultural huddle around the Frognal
Brook and a sprinkling of village ponds.

With all this water around, the most
likely of several explanations for the
ancient name of **FROGNAL** is 'the
place of frogs'. (Quite a few other frog
names scatter the country: 'Frognal' also
appears in Harrow and Chislehurst.)
The ponds survived the building of some
fine residences in upper Frognal during
the Spa period but with the development
of the lower end, which was not until the
1880s, all signs of farm life disappeared.
Earlier in the 19th century, a vicar of
Hampstead was saying he preferred 'the
open country of Frognal to the Town,
a place pervaded with a sense of culture
and sunshiny repose'.

Culture and repose are not now
obvious features of the Finchley Road
end of Frognal. But, in fact, the poet
Stephen Spender grew up in **No.10**
(now a part of **Heath Court**) and Home
Office pathologist Sir Bernard Spilsbury
found his final rest in 1947 at **No.20**
(part of an old-established hotel called
Langorf, which is Frognal in reverse).
Spender's autobiography, *World Within*

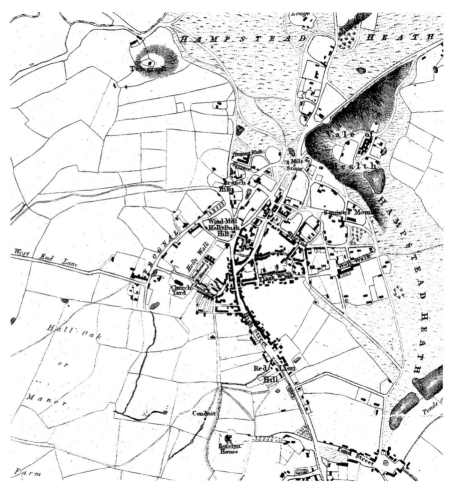

*1   Part of the map of Hampstead in 1814,
published with J J Park's Topography of
Hampstead.*

13

World, described his home as an 'ugly house in the Hampstead style, as if built from a box of bricks', and recalled his walk up the 'hill of red-brick Frognal' to the local school. We join him at the Wren-style **University College School**, designed by Arnold Mitchell and built by Dove Brothers – or, as the Latin inscription in the entrance puts it, 'Redemptoribus: Dove Fratribus'. A new hall roof and fibreglass cupola, replicas of the originals, followed the terrible fire of 1978. A public school for boys, founded in Gower Street in 1830, UCS moved to this unpromising site in 1907. Among other problems, here was the main source of the River Westbourne, which later heads for Kilburn and the Serpentine. The river still runs under the school in a specially-built crypt, where attempts have been made to grow mushrooms. The new building was opened by Edward VII (Fig 2), whose statue appears above the main door. Spenser Gate commemorates the reputedly fearsome headmaster at that time.

Opposite the school, there was much music-making in the 1950s. The opera-lovers of **Nos.31** and **31A** combined their gardens to make Hampstead's Open Air Theatre (orchestra pit in one garden, stage in the other), and Dennis Brain and his horn were based at **No.37, r**ecently blue plaqued. Another plaque on **No.39** shows that Kate Greenaway died here in 1901. At the height of her fame as a children's book illustrator, she had the fashionable and locally-living Norman Shaw design her this studio house in 1885. It was bought in 1961 by Hampstead Borough Council. Her name lives on in nearby Greenaway Gardens, on an annual medal for children's book artists, and on a block in Boundary Road, but her grave in Hampstead Cemetery is, at this moment, sadly forgotten and forlorn.

Higher up, on the site of two consecutive mansions called Frognal Priory, one a pseudo-Gothic pile (Fig 3), the other an 1881 house by Norman Shaw, is **Frognal Close**. This is a neat but not gaudy group of houses designed in 1937 by E L Freud, son of Sigmund and father of Clement and Lucian. **Nos.1,2,5&6** are Listed Buildings.

2 Opening of University College School, Frognal, by Edward VII, July 1907.

Nos.49 and 51 Frognal were built in 1895 by Sir Reginald Blomfield, architect of Lambeth Bridge and the Regent Street Quadrant. He lived in the upper house and Cobden-Sanderson, William Morris's typographical collaborator, in the other. (Note that houses in Frognal north of here were renumbered after World War II.) Across the road, until the 1920s, was Priory Lodge, where Dr Samuel Johnson stayed and wrote most of *The Vanity of Human Wishes*. He resorted to Hampstead on several occasions between 1748 and 1752, mainly to give his neurotic wife a breath of country air. 'One man can learn more in a journey by the Hampstead coach', he said, 'than another can in making the grand tour of Europe.' Above Priory Lodge, also until the 1920s, was the vast Frognal Hall, the home of Lord Chief Justice Alvanley until his death in 1804: his name survives in a nearby street.

The design of **No.66** by Connell, Ward and Lucas in 1938 caused a sensation. The New Zealand architects, pioneers of the Modern Movement, appeared to be cocking a snook at their neighbour, Blomfield, who joined in a howl of local protest. Nonetheless, what was then called 'the greatest abortion ever perpetrated' has been hailed as the best pre-war modern house in England: it is a II⋆ Listed Building.

Further modern buildings can be seen in the unadopted road **FROGNAL WAY**, which took over part of the Frognal Hall estate in 1924. Architectural historian Andrew Saint has called it 'the showpiece of inter-war Hampstead housing', and certainly nearly every house has something of interest. **No.4** has been typed by Pevsner as Hollywood Spanish-Colonial: note the curious 1934 plaque with what appears to be a flying monk. **No.5** was by and for Adrian Gilbert Scott, grandson of Sir George, in 1930, and **No.7** by Oswald Milne – the only architect to be mayor of Hampstead. The Sun House, **No.9**, by Maxwell Fry in 1935, has been much praised by modernists and is the only one of these house to be Listed (recently upgraded to II⋆). **No.20** was designed by R L Page in 1934 for Gracie Fields (see plaque) and her first husband, Archie Pitt: it was

3 Frognal Priory. Anonymous watercolour, c.1859.

originally called *Blue Tiles*, but the roof is now nearer green. Keeping a low profile, **No.22** is an ingenious in-fill by Philip Pank.

Back in Frognal, **No.88** (Frognal Lodge) is commended by Pevsner for its early-18th-century door canopy. The centre part of **No.94**, the Old Mansion, dates from about 1700. The wings were added in the 19th century in sympathetic style. The original garden stretched from Mount Vernon to Church Row, where a tollgate controlled access to Frognal. **No.102** is the pretty Edwardian Frognal Cottage by Amyan Champneys (son of Basil): this was once the home of popular songsters Anne Ziegler and Webster Booth. **Nos.104&106** are dated c.1760, while **Nos.108&110** go back to Queen Anne or earlier; they are among the oldest houses in Hampstead. In the 18th century they were joined together as a pub, variously called The Three Pigeons, Ye Pilgrim, The Windmill and The Duke of Cumberland. A niche for the pub sign can be seen on the north wall of No.110, Grove Cottage, which now shows a plaque to its most distinguished resident, E V Knox, poet and *Punch* editor, who lived here 1945–71. Should there not also be recognition for his wife Mary, daughter of E H Shepard, who has achieved fame as illustrator of *Mary Poppins*? A blue plaque there certainly

is at No.108 for the Diaghilev prima ballerina Tamara Karsavina, resident here in the 1950s. The pop star Sting lived here in the 1980s.

Across the road we see that the magical contralto Kathleen Ferrier has a plaque on Frognal Mansions, **No.97**, where she lived from 1942 until 1953, the year of her death. Among the mighty musicians who often climbed the fifty steps to her flat were Bliss, Barbirolli and Bruno Walter. Downhill from the Mansions is the charming old Bay Tree Cottage, **No.95**, probably the gardener's cottage of the house behind (once Bay Tree Lodge). **No.81** (The Oaks) 'started as a Georgian house' writes Pevsner, 'but was extravagantly embellished in 1902 with balconies and roof pavilion by George Hornblower'. **No.79** is a late-18th-century house onto which was grafted a bigger building with Italianate watchtower, also in 1902. The turreted **No.71** bears a plaque to Sir Harold Gillies, the pioneering plastic surgeon. **No.69** was the home of actor Anton Walbrook in the 1960s. **No.65** was designed in 1939 by and for the architect/gardener Barbara Acworth. When it changed hands (along with £1 million) in 1985, it was said to have the largest garden in Hampstead.

Climbing up the hill again, we find Frognal House, **No.99**, dating from about 1740. After the Crimean War it

was the Sailors' Orphan Girls' Home until 116 Fitzjohns Avenue was built for them in 1869. In World War II it became the home (1940–42) of General de Gaulle and his family, as the Hampstead Plaque confirms. The French Government struck a commemorative medal in 1977 mentioning De Gaulle's stay in 'Fragonal'. The General had his wife and three children with him here, and the whole household spoke French. At this time Winston Churchill referred to De Gaulle as 'the monster of Hampstead'. The house was bought by the Sisters of St Dorothy in 1968 as an international finishing school for girls.

Higher up, in a backwater from the main road, is a delightful group of houses, **Nos.103–109**, built by Henry Flitcroft about 1745. They were originally one house, Frognal Grove, centred on No.105, with wings either side and stables at No.109. Flitcroft was architect of several London churches, including St Giles-in-the-Fields, and he had a street near there named after him; but his offer to design a new parish church for Hampstead was refused, as he would not enter a competition for it. His Frognal house was sometimes known as Montagu House, as it was occupied by an eminent lawyer, Edward Montagu. It was later owned by Flitcroft's granddaughter, who married into the Street family. G E Street, architect of the Law Courts in the Strand, enlarged the house in the 1860s. At this time, shortly after the residence here of Dr White, Vicar of Hampstead, the house was used for Baptist meetings. The southern wing had by then been hived off and became Upper Frognal Lodge.

The most famous occupant at No.103 was Ramsay MacDonald, Britain's first Labour Prime Minister. His residence in this grand house from 1925 to 1937 was much criticised by his socialist supporters, but he said he needed room for his vast library. MacDonald shares a plaque, surprisingly not with his noteworthy son Malcolm, a top Commonwealth administrator, who also lived here, but with Donald Ogden Stewart, an Oscar-winning screenwriter, who came here as a refugee from McCarthyism in the 1950s. If you saw Chaplin or Hepburn or Thurber calling at 103 Frognal, that was why. When put up for sale in the 1970s, the old stables at No.109 included a 'Flitcroft fireplace', a heated pool and sauna, and a garage big enough for a Rolls. Offers for all this stabling were invited in the region of £97,500. **No.111** was added to Frognal Grove in the late 19th century as a further coach house, but has been upgraded to a desirable residence, with a fine array of metal sculpture out front.

Montagu Grove, the name of the Lime Walk planted here in the early 18th century, has featured in many old Hampstead pictures, notably in *As Happy as a King* by William Collins (father of Wilkie) at the Tate Gallery. All the houses here are Listed, including their walls and railings and the mounting block.

On the other side of Frognal, where new houses have recently sprung up, stood Hampstead's first workhouse, opened in 1729 in a derelict Tudor building (see *Camden History Review 4* for a graphic account). It survived until 1757, and some of the old house bricks are said to be incorporated in the present garden wall. A later, grander workhouse was built in New End, much to the relief of the superior fraternity in Frognal.

At the top of the hill, **FROGNAL RISE** consists of a house of that name, entered formerly from Frognal but now from Lower Terrace (p 34), and **Nos.2&4**, which have been converted from stables into Spanish-style villas. Dating from the early 19th century, Frognal Rise was enlarged and embellished with *art nouveau* in the 1880s. For many years it was the home of stockbroker Herbert Marnham, a leading local Baptist and philanthropist (see Grove Place, p 31). He was Mayor of Hampstead in 1925 and received the freedom of the borough in 1934.

Across the road, **OAK HILL WAY** has a sign saying 'Private Road', but it is in fact a very old right-of-way. The only old house on it is **Combe Edge**, built in 1874. The red plaque shows that its original owner was Elizabeth Rundle Charles, author of a once-popular children's book with the formidable title *The Chronicles of the Schönberg Cotta Family*.

We follow this rustic route to **OAK HILL PARK**, which was first developed around 1851 and won a Great Exhibition design award for gentlemen's dwellings. Most of the houses had gone by 1961, when the new development by Michael Lyell Associates won a Civic Trust Award. The oaks which once covered this hill were called North Wood, but they were cut down in 1470, except for fifty trees which the monks insisted be left. Few oaks remain today, but there is a block of flats called **Northwood Lodge** where Peter Sellers occupied the penthouse in 1962. Local architect Ted Levy redesigned the flat as a Hollywood apartment, but the actor called it his 'Hampstead Torture Chamber' and left later the same year. (He also left his wife Anne, who married Ted Levy the following year.) The poet Gerard Manley Hopkins enjoyed climbing the trees when his family lived in Oak Hill Park in the 1850s, but the house has gone, as have the others where

St Margaret's School originated, and where Sir William Rothenstein lived (see Church Row, p 78). Hopkins is commemorated, however, by a plaque on a house in the south-west corner, **Oak Hill House**. This is one of the two survivals from the 1850s, and was one of several houses hereabouts visited by Florence Nightingale in search of fresh-air treatment.

No.1, at the Frognal end, is the other original, and during the 1930s was the home of publisher Sir Geoffrey Faber. According to Peter Ackroyd's biography of T S Eliot, the poet visited Faber every Wednesday evening in 1940 and slept in his basement bomb shelter. At this time another successful publisher, Sir Stanley Unwin, was living in Oak Hill Park and, undeterred by the bombs, he stayed on until his death in 1968. After the war he bought the 7-acre estate from the Neave family–to avoid, as he wrote in *The Truth about a Publisher*, 'losing my house and my tennis court': he had **No.4** built for himself beside the tennis court. The architects were also Michael Lyell Associates.

We cross over Frognal to **FROGNAL GARDENS**, which was developed around 1890 over the garden of the Old Mansion. The main architect was James Neale, a pupil of G E Street, and the builders were the local firm of Allison & Foskett. **No.20** was designed

by and for Henry Ashley, who was to win the competition for the Freemasons' Hall in the 1930s. His local architecture includes the columbarium in the parish churchyard extension. Nearly invisible up a driveway, **No.18**, Frognal End, was built for Sir Walter Besant in 1892. Of the two official plaques on the house, one is for Besant, who has a street named after him in West Hampstead and whose grave in the parish churchyard is Listed – all of which goes to show that this forgotten novelist and antiquary was once somebody. The house was occupied in the 1920s by Lord Pentland, Governor of Madras, and from the 1940s by Labour leader Hugh Gaitskell, to whom the second plaque refers. When Chancellor of the Exchequer in 1950, he even rejected 11 Downing Street in favour of 18 Frognal Gardens. He too is buried in the parish churchyard. Residents at **No.16** have ranged from Sir Alexander Butterworth, Director of Welwyn Garden City Ltd in the 1930s, to Bernice Rubens, Booker Prize winner in 1970. About this time **No.1a**, a Roman-style villa, was the home of financial wizard Sir Paul Chambers: his many achievements included chairmanship of ICI (now Zeneca) and the origination of the PAYE system of taxation. Other notable residents in this road have included the actor Alastair Sim, at **No.8**, the

economist Lord Balogh at **No.12** and poet Eva Gore-Booth at **No.14**. Several buildings on the eastern side have, as Pevsner says, 'a variety of playful gables'.

Back down Frognal we turn right into **FROGNAL LANE**, the old route to the village of West End (round West End Green). Until 1895 it was part of West End Lane, and was still rural (Fig 4). The houses at the Frognal end are on the site of the old manorial buildings, as the names suggest. The attractive **Nos.19&21**, Maryon Hall and Maryon House, a semi-detached pair built as one house around 1793, recall the Maryon Wilson family, Lords of the Manor since the 18th century. Maryon Hall was commended by the novelist Maria Edgeworth, who visited 'delicious Frognal' in 1819 and enjoyed its 'cultivated taste and cheerful tempers'. No.21 was the home for many years of Luigi Denza, the last mayor of Hampstead and a champion of Social Services: he died in 1991, aged 99. **No.23**, Old Frognal Court, has a plaque (not visible from the street) saying it was erected by Sir T S Wilson in 1785. Before it was much altered in the 1920s, the house was called The Ferns and belonged to the Prance family, great benefactors of Christ Church and St Stephen's.

In a side road opposite, **Hall Oak** uses the name of the Manor Farm on this site. The sturdy house was built for himself by Basil Champneys, which explains the lettering on the date plaque, 'AD 1881 BC'. Champneys was architect also of Newnham College and other Oxbridge buildings. His local contributions include Oak Tree House in Redington Gardens and two St Luke's churches, one in Kidderpore Avenue and one in Kentish Town. Nearby **No.40**, Manor Lodge, was built about 1813 for the manorial bailiff. As late as the 1920s, the *Ham&High* was reporting that 'the summer meeting of the Court Leet and Court Baron of the Manor of Hampstead is held at Manor Lodge, Frognal'. The wonderful actress Dame Peggy Ashcroft lived here for 40 years from 1946. Sir Alan Cobham, the champion aviator, lived at **No.22** around 1930.

4   The Frognal Lane area, looking towards Kilburn, watercolour by Harold Lawes, 1890.

Branching off Frognal Lane, **LANGLAND GARDENS** first sprouted houses in the 1890s. **No.21** has a plaque to proclaim the birthplace of Cecil Beaton, photographer of the famous and designer, among other delights, of *My Fair Lady*. His family moved here in 1904, the year of his birth, because they 'considered the air so much healthier for growing children'. In *My Bolivian Aunt*, Beaton remembered this 'small, tall redbrick house of ornate but indiscriminate Dutch style', but preferred the grander house they moved to in Templewood Avenue in 1911. His memories of Heath Mount School in Heath Street were not altogether happy as another pupil, Evelyn Waugh no less, stuck pins into him. Waugh's *Little Learning* records that he was suitably flogged for his crime.

Langland Gardens seems to be a strictly fanciful street name, but its neighbour **LINDFIELD GARDENS** commemorates a village on the Maryon Wilson estates in Sussex, not far from Nutley and Maresfield. **No.15** was the first married home in the 1950s of Leon Garfield, now a leading children's author but then a biochemist at Whittington Hospital, Highgate.

Back into Frognal Lane and down to Finchley Road, we come to **St Andrew's Church**, which has been a pillar of Presbyterianism since 1904.

In fact, there has been a Presbyterian presence in Hampstead since 1662 and it dominated the early years of Rosslyn Hill Chapel. In 1844 the congregation rented the Temperance Hall in Perrins Court, and in 1853 took over the old Long Room by Gainsborough Gardens. In 1862 they built Trinity Chapel in Willoughby Road and, exactly 100 years later, they pulled most of it down and migrated to St Andrew's. They were united here with the Congregationalists in 1972 and became 'the largest, liveliest dissenting congregation in the area'. The junction of Frognal Lane and Finchley Road is generally thought to be where *The Woman in White* first met the hero of Wilkie Collins's novel, published in 1859. A 1980 television version could capture the remote rurality of this scene only by filming in deepest Suffolk.

Back uphill to the north of Frognal Lane, three house-proud roads were developed early in the 20th century. The first we come to is **BRACKNELL GARDENS**, which was named after a Maryon Wilson estate in Berkshire. **No.16** (with blue plaque) was the home of Leonard Huxley until his death in 1933. He wrote a notable biography of his father, T H Huxley, and also produced three famous sons: Julian, Aldous, and the Nobel prizewinner Andrew. Aldous was living here from 1917 until his marriage and consequent

move to Hampstead Hill Gardens two years later. Sir Julian came to live in Pond Street in 1943. The eminent psychoanalyst Melanie Klein also spent her last years at No.16, dying there in 1960. She specialised in children's subconscious and explored what Freud called 'the dim and shadowy era' of early childhood.

To the north, **GREENAWAY GARDENS**, which grew over the grounds of an estate known as Frognal Park around 1914, honours the memory of Kate Greenaway (see No.39 Frognal, p 14). When the superstitiously-numbered **12a** was sold in 1970 to the Government of Trinidad and Tobago for its High Commissioner, it sported a heated log cabin in its extensive grounds. Further up, **CHESTERFORD GARDENS**, named after a Maryon Wilson estate in Essex, also covered part of Frognal Park. The pseudo-timbered **No.18** was the last home of Henry Holiday, the artist (see Redington Gardens, p 22); he died here in 1927.

To the north of Chesterford Gardens, **REDINGTON ROAD** originated in 1875, when the Maryon Wilsons began selling off their Hampstead estates. The origin of the street name is unknown. It would be nice to think it commemorated the 14th-century Prior Redington of the Order of

St John, which held land near here (see Templewood Avenue, p 22), but it more probably salutes the distinguished Irish administrator Sir Thomas Redington. The main developer, George Washington Hart, had strong Irish connections.

Hart's principal architect was C H B Quennell, perhaps more widely known as the author (with his wife Marjorie) of the series *A History of Everyday Things in England*. Quennell, according to Alastair Service in *Victorian and Edwardian Hampstead*, 'produced series after series of excellent designs, with occasional larger houses of spectacular inventiveness'. Together, Hart and Quennell built over 100 high-quality houses in this part of Hampstead, which they confusingly called the West Hampstead Estate. The Redington area was fulsomely praised by an estate agent's blurb of 1932: 'The favoured Western Slopes are sheltered... A warm and genial climate has earned for the locality the name of the Madeira of Hampstead'.

The houses at the Frognal end came first. **Nos.2 and 4** were designed in 1876 by William Morris's associate Philip Webb – 'with quiet cleverness and curiosities' says Andrew Saint: they are now Listed II. No.2 was for many years the home of the distinguished architect John Brandon-Jones, and No.4 that of

F R D'O Monro, long-time Clerk of the Hampstead Wells & Campden Trust. The 'unrepentantly Gothic' **No.6**, by T K Green, was built as the vicarage of the parish church (St John-at-Hampstead), also in 1876. Stained glass on the ground floor used to show St John and a picture of the church. **No.16** is basically by Arts-and-Craftsman A H Mackmurdo in 1889, but extended by local architect Maxwell Ayrton in the 1920s. An early resident was Sir Hamo Thornycroft, sculptor of, for instance, General Gordon in Trafalgar Square. In the 1920s came civil engineer Sir Owen Williams, responsible for building Wembley Stadium and the M1 motorway, and in the 1970s actors John Alderton and Pauline Collins. Another star of *Upstairs, Downstairs*, Gordon Jackson, lived at **No.36**, and master showman Lord Bernard Delfont lived at **No.42A**.

On the opposite side, **Nos.35–37** were built by Horace Field (see Rosslyn Hill, p 72) and called Redington Lodge. In the late 1930s this was the home of LSE sociologist Professor Morris Ginsberg. At the corner with Oak Hill Avenue, **No.39** can be enjoyed for its fancy turret and the pargeted swans in its eaves.

OAK HILL AVENUE, originally Barby Avenue, has had two resident mountaineers of note – Christian

Bonington and Elizabeth Schwarzkopf. The latter, who lived at **No.3** in the 1950s with her husband Walter Legge, is more famous for scaling the heights of opera, but mountaineering appeared in her *Who's Who* list of recreations. **Nos.21–27** have all been Listed.

No.45 Redington Road was frequently under attack by protesting mobs in 1962–64, when its occupant Henry Brooke was Home Secretary. Councillor Brooke rose from the Hampstead Borough Council in 1936 to the LCC in 1945 and to Parliament as Hampstead's Conservative MP from 1950 to 1966. When Labour briefly won Hampstead in 1966, he left the area and became Baron Brooke of Cumnor. Higher up are two architecturally notable houses, **No.81** by Sir Edward Maufe, designer of Guildford Cathedral, and the hilly **No.87**, built in 1938 by Oliver Hill: 'good, asymmetrical, redbrick villa in strictly modern forms' writes Pevsner, who also logs the gardens by Christopher Tunnard.

Back on the east side, **Nos.54&56** by Quennell have both recently been Listed. The quirky **No.66** was built in 1910 by Dr William Garnett and given the jabberwocky name of The Wabe. He was an ardent fan of Lewis Carroll, as well as education adviser to the LCC.

Lewis Carroll was one of many distinguished visitors to **Oak Tree**

House in **REDINGTON GARDENS**. Designed by Basil Champneys (see Frognal Lane, p 19) in 1874 for Henry Holiday, the house was originally approached from Branch Hill. This eminent Hampstead Victorian (see *Camden History Review* 6) specialised in stained glass – samples can be seen in Westminster Abbey and Rosslyn Hill Chapel – and established his own glassworks at 20 Church Row, where he claimed to have found the secret of fine blues in medieval glass. Apart from Carroll, who asked Holiday to illustrate *The Hunting of the Snark*, Gladstone came here to a Home Rule garden party, Sylvia Pankhurst to a suffragette meeting, and all the leading Pre-Raphaelites to discuss art. His wife Catherine was one of William Morris's chief embroiderers. All this was in Oak Tree House, once a cultural centre, now highly desirable Council flats.

We turn north into **TEMPLEWOOD GARDENS** and **AVENUE,** which were laid out about 1910 and include some handsome houses by Quennell. The streets were named after two local farms, Great and Little Templewood, which were probably once owned by the Knights Templar. Cecil Beaton's family (see also p 20) lived at **No.1** Templewood Avenue, then called Temple Court, from 1911 to 1922. Many houses in

this area have become ambassadorial residences and homes of show-business personalities, including Danny La Rue. At the corner with West Heath Road, **Heath Park Gardens** were erected in 1988, offering apartments at up to £4 million each; their cantilevered balconies are 'aggressively flamboyant', says Pevsner. To the east of Templewood Avenue are **GRANGE GARDENS** and **BIRCHWOOD DRIVE**, developed from the mid-1980s on the sites of two old estates, the grounds of The Grange and of Spedan Tower. A black plaque to the memory of store-founder John Lewis of Spedan Tower (p 35) is located here.

We now go south across Redington Road to **HEATH DRIVE**, where Quennell also designed many of the imposing houses. This road was first developed in 1890, under the more suitable name of West Hampstead Avenue. **Nos.24–26** and **31–33** have recently been Listed. Local residents have included Thomas J Wise, the greatest of all literary forgers. In 1910, when Wise came to **No.25**, his book collection was considered supreme, but in 1934 many were revealed as forgeries. The typographer Stanley Morison (see Hollyberry Lane, p 32) was instrumental in unmasking him. After Wise died here in 1937, his Ashley Library, forgeries or no, was sold to the British Museum. **No.6** was the home of the distinguished

Dr David Pitt, who was born on an estate in Grenada called Hampstead: he became a Labour Life Peer, Lord Pitt of Hampstead, and died here in 1994. On the opposite side of the road is a small green and a narrow alley called **Bracknell Way**.

Adjoining this part of Heath Drive, **KIDDERPORE AVENUE** was also laid out in 1890, mostly over the carriageway to the stately **Kidderpore Hall**, which has survived at the top of the hill. The original hall (architect, T Howard) was built in 1843 by John Teil, an East India merchant with tanneries in the Kidderpore district of Calcutta. The northern part of his estate was bought in the 1850s for a reservoir, and the rest was acquired by Westfield College in 1890. The college, which originated in Maresfield Gardens in 1882 as the Girton of North London, moved to East London in 1992, leaving behind some fine buildings designed by Sir Hugh Casson and others. Westfield's name is perpetuated in the new blocks of luxury apartments currently (1999) going up. Kidderpore Hall belongs at present to the Spiro Institute. Many of the other buildings are used by King's College as a 'student village'. **No.19** is the home of the Hampstead School of Art. At the west end of the Avenue, **No.14** has a delightfully quirky façade. Artist George Swinstead built the house in 1901. Since World War II it has been the home of the musical Craxton family. Harold Craxton and his daughter Janet, the oboeist, taught for many years at the Royal Academy of Music; they created the Craxton Memorial Trust and the Craxton Prize to help young musicians.

St Luke's Church next door was built in 1899, with a touch of Arts and Crafts, by Basil Champneys (see also p 19). Apart from the castellated doorways, you can enjoy the whole frontage which, as Alastair Service says, 'fizzes with delectable stone carvings'. Note the ox on the weathervane, which is St Luke's logo. The vicarage, **No.12**, was also by Champneys and has now been Listed. At the other end of the Avenue, **No.7** was for many years the home of James Gunn RA, painter of many official portraits, including George VI and our present Queen: he died here in 1965. Opposite his house, **No.4** is surprisingly Tudorised and splendidly decorated with grotesques and other mouldings. The date 1900 is on the front and the colourful tympanum over the corner door must not be missed. Cinema pioneer Jonas Wolfe lived here in the 1940s.

KIDDERPORE GARDENS originated in the 1890s, but was called Cecilia Road until about 1907. St Margaret's School came to **No.18** from Oak Hill Park after World War II. The school was founded in 1884 'for the daughters of gentlepeople', who later included Sir Gerald du Maurier's literary daughters Angela and Daphne. In the 1980s **No.4** was the home and office of a 'mysterious millionaire publisher', according to the *Ham&High*, who made a fortune from compiling and printing the first crossword magazine *The Puzzler*.

We return via Kidderpore Avenue to **PLATT'S LANE**, which was named after Thomas Pell Platt, builder of Child's Hill House on a site near the junction with Rosecroft Avenue. Platt was an oriental scholar whose main claim to fame was translating the Bible into Ethiopian. This cannot have contributed much to the cost of the enormous house, grounds and farm which he owned, and where he died in 1852. The estate was sold up at the turn of the century. **No.8** is now the most interesting house in the road, being a characteristic long, low building by C F A Voysey, a pioneer of the Modern Movement. He built it for his father in 1896 (date on drainpipe) and it was, writes Pevsner, 'astonishingly ahead of its date'. The original name, Annesley Lodge (one of Voysey's Christian names was Annesley), is visible on the west wall. The house is now divided up. **Nos.14 and 16** are marked 'West Middlesex Waterworks 1806', but the date has been corrected below to the more likely 1875, which is when the huge reservoir was built here. In 1993 the cottages were saved from a developer's bid to build flats on the site, after a Department of the Environment Inquiry. The inspector admitted that the houses had no architectural merit and were 'at odds with the Edwardian character of the area but. . .this created an element of surprise' and contributed to 'the rich diversity of the urban environment'. Opposite, **No.21** has a private plaque to Thomas Masaryk, first president of Czechoslovakia, who lived here in exile during World War I and planned the liberation of his country. **No.65** was the home of Ballard Berkeley (the major in *Fawlty Towers*) and **No.69**, actually on the Hendon side of the parish boundary, that of German film star Conrad Veidt. Platt's Lane was once known as Duval's Lane, after a notorious 17th-century highwayman, and this name was later corrupted into Devil's Lane. Bible-thumping Mr Platt put an end to all that.

To the east of Platt's Lane, **FERNCROFT**, **HOLLYCROFT** and **ROSECROFT AVENUES** had their names officially approved in 1896, and the streets were developed over the meadows of Platt's Farm by the busy builder George Hart: it was he who devised these fanciful names, and he again used Quennell as his architect. A tributary of the River Westbourne (see also p 14) rises near here and crosses Ferncroft Avenue close to where **Croftway**, an old right of way, leads down to Finchley Road. Several houses in Ferncroft Avenue have recently been Listed: **Nos.6–8, 12–14, 26–26A, 33–35, 40–42**. One of the few not by Quennell, the tile-hung **No.25**, has kept its decorative bargeboards.

In Hollycroft Avenue, **No.46** was designed in 1907 by Sir Guy Dawber, noted for his houses in the Cotswolds and Hampstead Garden Suburb. **Nos.43–49** have now been Listed. **No.28** was the last home of Leslie Brooke, father of Henry and illustrator of the popular *Johnny Crow* series. He died in 1940 and would have been glad to know that he was buried by the High Street undertaker, J Crowe. Quennell appears again in Rosecroft Avenue at the heavily shuttered **No.20**, Croft House, which he designed in 1898. The same date can be seen in the eaves of **No.18**, together with some naked nymphs. The sculpted façade of **No.17** is also worth viewing. Both these houses and **No.20** have now been Listed. Cartoonist Gerald Scarfe was living at the turreted **No.1** in the 1960s

West of Platt's Lane, most of **BRIARDALE** and **CLORANE GARDENS** were also creations of Hart and Quennell in the late 1890s. The former street name seems to be merely fanciful but Clorane, not being euphonious, may commemorate a country seat of that name in Limerick.

At the north end of Platt's Lane, **TELEGRAPH HILL** is named after the signalling station based here during the Napoleonic wars. Originally serving the Duke of York's headquarters, the station became a vital link between the Admiralty and Yarmouth from 1808 to 1814; it used a shutter semaphore system. The present road was built in the 1930s, and those who remember the pianist and composer Billy Mayerl will like to know that he had a house here in the 1940s called *Marigold*, the title of his greatest hit.

Round the corner, **WEST HEATH ROAD** follows a very old track from Hampstead village to Child's Hill. At the corner with Platt's Lane is the imposing **Sarum Chase**, 'unashamedly Hollywood Tudor' according to Pevsner. It was built in 1932 for artist Frank Salisbury (hence 'Sarum') by his nephew Vyvyan, and was much frequented by royalty and politicians for portrait sittings. The house now belongs to the School of Economic Science. Several large c.1900 houses along the road have kept their old names – the well-turreted **No.13** (now Listed) has *Ashmount* on one gate pillar and mysteriously *Lipa* on the other. (Lipa is a place-name found in former Yugoslavia and the Philippines.) The well-walled Tudorish **No.11** is still called *Middleheath*. In contrasting style, **No.9** by James Gowan is, some say, 'one of the finest modern houses in Hampstead'. Built in 1962–4, its stark exterior is excused by Pevsner as being 'from the brief period when the austerity of the Brutalist aesthetic was in the ascendant'. Between here and Branch Hill, an area much redeveloped in the 1980s, was The Grange, once the home of flamboyant actor-manager Sir Herbert Beerbohm Tree. He abandoned it in 1891 because of the problems of getting transport to 'such a remote country spot'. A black plaque salutes him and another actor, Wilson Barrett, at the entrance to **MANSION GARDENS**, which together with Grange Gardens (p 22) resulted from the Grange redevelopment. The plaque also records Constable's first painting of Branch Hill Pond, which included a house called The Salt Box on the site of The Grange.

Route 2
The Grove
From Holly Hill
to Branch Hill

*Start at Hampstead Tube station
and climb Holly Hill.*

The emblem of the old Hampstead Vestry, forerunner of the Borough Council, was a sprig of holly, and the west side of **HOLLY HILL** had a grove of hollies until the 1940s. But in the 18th century this road was called Cloth Hill, which suggests that some of the

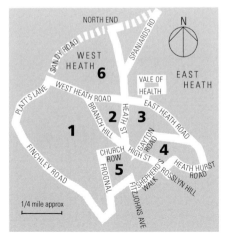

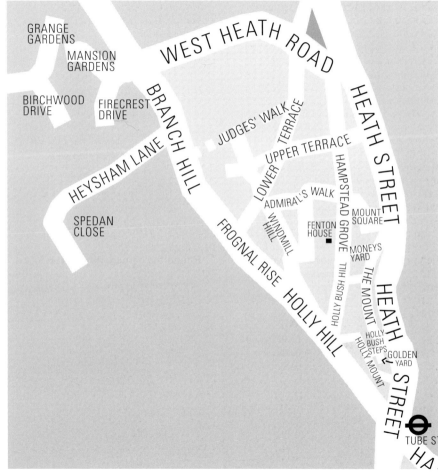

many local laundresses were hanging out their washing on the holly bushes. Certainly the road follows an ancient track, much lowered over the years by digging from surrounding sandpits. The raised path on the west side has old railings and bollards dated 1828, which are Listed.

Behind the western wall is the Junior Branch of **University College School** (see p 14), established in 1891, 16 years before their seniors came to Hampstead. Their original building, dating from 1665, was demolished in 1927, but its outline has been preserved in an ornamental garden, and its front door, staircase and some panelling have also been incorporated in the new school. Among the staff here early in the 20th century was the poet James Elroy Flecker; he started the library but was otherwise not a success. The actor Dirk Bogarde, however, succeeded in establishing a drama club when he was a pupil here in the 1930s.

On the same side, **Nos.15–19** have been converted from an early 18th-century farmhouse. Tradition has it that this was connected with one of the windmills of Windmill Hill (p 32), and that part of it was the granary. Confusingly, **Nos.12&14** are jointly

called Granary House, for reasons unknown: this early-19th-century building (much altered in 1951) has been used by builders, sheet-metal workers and, in the 1920s, as Holly

School, a rival preparatory school to UCS. The picturesque houses **Nos.16–24** are basically early- to mid-19th-century with later additions, such as the sundial on No.18. All the above

5   *Drawing of Holly Hill in 1928 by E Stamp.*

houses have been Listed, as have the garages higher up; these are 18th-century brick vaults, linked with the houses in Holly Mount (see below) and supporting their gardens. Before the age of the car, they were used as workshops, a greengrocer's and a florist's.

The name **HOLLY BUSH HILL** used to include all Holly Hill as well, but now embraces only a grassy triangle and five handsome Listed houses. **No.1**, Alpine Cottage, is early-19th-century, but the others are mid- or late-18th-century, some with spear-and-pineapple railings. White and weatherboarded, **Romney's House** has a blue plaque to salute the artist's residence here. This was originally the stables of a house in The Mount behind, which George Romney (Fig 6) bought in 1796. But his efforts to convert them into a house, studio and Palace of Art broke his health, and in 1799 he returned to his neglected wife in Kendal.

In 1807 the building was enlarged for Assembly Rooms, with money raised by a tontine lottery, and became a cultural centre for Hampstead, the Burgh House of its day. Here was held in 1829 the first Heath Protection meeting, chaired by James Fenton of Fenton House, and here in 1833 was given a notable series of lectures by such authorities as Faraday, Constable and Elizabeth Fry. In the 1880s, when the new Town Hall in Haverstock Hill had taken away the assembly business, first the Liberals, then the Constitutional Club moved in. This continued until the 1920s, when the last beneficiary of the tontine died and the house could be sold. From 1929 until 1939 it belonged to Clough Williams-Ellis, architect of Portmeirion, who had it 'much altered and adapted to our curious habits', as he wrote in *Architect Errant*. The house is now divided up but the splendid pilastered assembly room has survived.

Around 1900 Holly Bush Hill was planned as the Hampstead station on the proposed Charing Cross, Euston and Hampstead Underground Railway. Powers were sought to widen approach roads and also to open a station on the West Heath. Protesters put a stop to that idea.

Round the corner in **HOLLY MOUNT**, the **Holly Bush Tavern** was also converted from stables and, from 1807, was linked to the Assembly Rooms, originally as their catering wing. The pub has miraculously resisted modernisation in recent years and, among its snug nooks and old wooden panels, are fine displays of etched glass. Many of the houses in this extraordinarily complex cul-de-sac are 18th-century, but the street name is not used in the Rate Books until the 1830s. Earlier, this jumbled area came under the heading of 'Nagg's Head Side', after the pub in Heath Street.

The 1851 Census showed a good social mix here, including eleven servants and four laundresses. **Nos.1&2** were then one house, occupied by octogenarian Lady Mary Bentham, sister-in-law of Jeremy. **Nos.5–8**, recognisable on the 1762 Manor Map, are early examples of back-to-back

6 *George Romney (self-portrait, c.1780).*

housing. Entry to **Nos.7&8** is down a side path, from which there is a good view of No.4's attractive rear. **Nos.14&15** are mid-18th-century. The popular actress Dame Anna Neagle was living at No.14 in the late 1930s. The nearly invisible **No.16**, once Alma Cottage, is partly built on top of a house in Golden Yard (see below). **No.17** was the first Baptist Chapel in Hampstead, built in 1818. In 1860 it became the printing works of the *Ham&High* and later the *Hampstead Record*, while from 1911 it was an artist's studio. Note the weathervane on **No.18**, which was a beer shop in the 1830s, the Holly Mount Laundry in the 1850s, and a lodging house at the turn of the century. Holly Bush House, **No.21**, was the home for many years of Donald and Catherine Carswell, close friends of D H Lawrence, who liked to lodge here. Donald, a barrister, checked *Women in Love* for libel; Catherine helped type *Lady Chatterley's Lover*.

Of the two eastern exits from Holly Mount, the further one is anonymous, though once identified as Cock Alley for convenience; the other is the attractive **Holly Bush Steps**, which lead down to **GOLDEN YARD**. The name of this picturesque backwater does not appear in the Rate Books until 1831, being previously given as Gouldings Yard. The Goulding family owned much property hereabouts. The yard's history, going back to the 16th century, has been traced by a local resident and summarised on a display board here. **No.4** is the house supporting 16 Holly Mount (see above); the occupant of the former had once to complain to the latter about coal falling from her cellar into his attic. **Nos.1,7&8** are Listed, the last two being basically 18th-century.

At the bottom of the steps we turn left into **THE MOUNT**, which has many 18th-century houses and two major artistic connections. The first is Romney's residence at **No.6**, Cloth Hill (Listed II). This was built as two houses in 1694, the year after Fenton House, but was rapidly made into one dwelling. As the daughter of the house married Andrew Pitt, who is known to have entertained Voltaire in Hampstead, it seems likely that the great philosopher came here. The house was divided again in 1801 and, at the end of the 19th century, the main part (old No.5) was the family home of publisher Edward Bell; the remainder was The Mount School. The garden wall and gate, which are Listed, can be seen in Ford Madox Brown's famous picture *Work*–the street's other claim to artistic fame. (Versions of the painting are in Manchester and Birmingham galleries, and one is reproduced with commentary in *Camden History Review 2*.) The Pre-Raphaelite Madox Brown began the picture in 1852, inspired by seeing navvies at work on Hampstead's main drainage. **No.11**, Caroline House, and **No.12**, Holly Cottage, are also visible in the background of *Work*, and Madox Brown lodged at the latter in 1883, when recovering from a violent attack of gout. Before this time, No.11 belonged to Mrs Margaret Money and this enclave off The Mount, including attractive **St Helen's Cottage**, became known as **Money's Yard**. To the south, **No.4** (Bentham House) was the home of comedian Dudley Moore around 1970. This end of the street was called Elba Place on the 1835 map, while the northern stretch was shown as Mount Pleasant.

The 1851 Rate Book called the whole road Silver Street (this stayed until 1936), and **THE MOUNT SQUARE** at the top of the road was known as Golden Square. Caroline White commented sourly on all these precious titles in 1903: 'There is nothing in their present appearance except irony to suggest the etymology of the names.' But fortunes have changed and the square is no longer the slum that Daphne du Maurier described in one of her family biographies. **Nos.7&8** were respectively the laundry and the stables of Old Grove House, to which there is an attractive back entrance. **Nos.10–16** are 18th-century, the last one being used by a veterinary surgeon and later a farrier, right up to World War I. Note the horseshoe on the gate.

Across Hampstead Grove (see below) is the so-called **ADMIRAL'S WALK**. Originally included in The Grove, the street was given its present name in 1949 to connect with its main residence, **Admiral's House**, dating from 1700. Until recently, this was thought to have been the home of 18th-century Admiral Matthew Barton. But, as an article in *Camden History Review 9* revealed, he was living in Rosslyn Hill all the time, and the highest rank associated with the house was that of a mere lieutenant. It was Lieutenant Fountain North who lived here from 1775 until his death in 1811 and adapted the roof to look like the deck of a ship; he even installed a couple of cannon up there, which he fired to celebrate naval victories. The residence here of architect-extraordinary Sir George Gilbert Scott is well authenticated by the official plaque. During his stay here (1856–64) he was working on plans for the Albert Memorial, and he also designed a gallery for the local Christ Church (p 46). It is a curiosity that this champion of Gothic Revival and the only begetter of St Pancras Station Hotel should have taken this sober-sided house and should not have left his mark on

the building. Among other eminent occupants here have been the army historian Sir John Fortescue, who was ironically the first to call it Admiral's House, and his wife Winifred, author of *There's Rosemary, There's Rue*. The best of Constable's three paintings of this house is at the Tate Gallery.

Grove Lodge, attached to Admiral's House, is of about the same age, and also bears an official plaque. This notes that John Galsworthy lived here from 1918 to 1933, his years of fame. During this time he completed *The Forsyte Saga*, and in 1932 he won the Nobel Prize for Literature. As he was too ill to collect his prize, a delegation came to Grove Lodge to deliver it. Behind is a picturesque Gothic villa of early 19th-century origins called **Terrace Lodge**. Opposite, **No.13**, called Broadside, is praised by Pevsner as a 'crisply designed, well-detailed house of 1960'.

In his *Table Book* of 1827, William Hone called Hampstead 'the place of groves', and so it has remained. There are still enough fine old trees in **HAMPSTEAD GROVE** to justify the name. From its first mention in the Rate Books of 1831, it was just 'The Grove', and the name sometimes embraced parts of Upper and Lower Terrace, as well as Admiral's Walk and even Admiral's House. To avoid confusion with The Grove in Highgate, the name was

changed to Hampstead Grove in 1937.

Towards Whitestone Pond, a grassy bank conceals Hampstead's first **reservoir**, built in 1856 by the New River Company. Here also is the Meteorological Station and **observatory** of the Hampstead Scientific Society, which is open at some weekends for star-gazing, 'if the sky is clear' (see the notice).

Among the neo-Georgian houses on the right, **No.32** was for many years the home of Lord Cottesloe, whose chairmanships ranged from Tate Gallery to Battersea Dogs' Home, and his name is well known at the National Theatre. Nearby is **New Grove House**, of the 18th century but 'stuccoed and Tudorised', as Pevsner put it, around 1840. Here, as the red plaque shows, lived the writer and artist George du Maurier from 1874 to 1895, the year before his death. His granddaughter Daphne has written much about his life, and there is some autobiographical detail in his novels *Peter Ibbetson* and *Trilby*, the latter famous for the odious character Svengali. The former includes scenes in Hampstead, as did du Maurier's famous *Punch* cartoons. Adjoining is **No.6**, the early-18th-century Old Grove House, with the highest roof terrace in London. When the garden front was rebuilt in the 1950s, all old windows blocked up because (presumably) of the window tax were carefully re-blocked in identical fashion. Hampstead's second windmill is thought to have been located near here.

Across the road is the oldest surviving mansion in Hampstead, **Fenton House**, built about 1693. The date was found on a chimney. Early in the 18th century, this was called Ostend House and was owned by a silk merchant, Joshua Gee. His initials once appeared on the handsome wrought-iron gates by Tijou, giving on to Holly Bush Hill. Gee had close connections with the American colonies, traded with George Washington's father, imported pig-iron from Maryland and was an original Pennsylvanian mortgagee. In 1793 the property, then known as The Clock House (see dial over door), was bought by Philip Fenton, a Riga merchant, who left it to his nephew, James. The latter added the loggia and new entrance on the east side. Fenton House, together with its beautiful contents and splendid walled garden, was bequeathed by Lady Binning in 1952 to the National Trust, and should be visited for its pictures, porcelain and furniture, as well as the Benton Fletcher collection of musical instruments. (These were originally housed in Old Devonshire House, near Queen Square, which was destroyed during World War II.) The pride of the collection is a 1612 harpsichord once used by Handel.

On the east side of the Grove are six attractive cottages, **Nos.4–14**, nearly 200 years old. 13th-century tiles have been found in the basement of one cottage, and praying shells, as used by medieval travellers, in the walls of another. Could there have been lodgings on this site for Westminster monks visiting their Hampstead estates? Two leading artists of the London Group lived in this row for many years – Brian Robb at No.10 and Ethelbert White at No.14. The writer Mary Webb came to No.12 in 1923, enjoying some scant literary success, but frequently unwell and unhappy. Among other things her husband Henry, a master at King Alfred's, was having an affair with a pupil. She completed *Precious Bane* here in 1924, but it was not until 3 years later, after praise from Prime Minister Stanley Baldwin, that the book finally brought her fame; in that same year she died. The success of *Precious Bane* allowed Henry to give up teaching and marry his pupil.

Across the green of Holly Bush Hill is **MOUNT VERNON**, named after General Charles Vernon, an aide-de-camp to George III, who owned land here around 1800. 'It must have been a perfect spot', writes Pevsner of the green, 'before **Mount Vernon** broke the spell and dwarfed all the rest by its pretentious mass'. The main chateau-like building was designed by Roger Smith in 1880 as the North London Hospital for Consumption (Fig 7). This was much enlarged over the years, including a western extension by local architect Maxwell Ayrton: he also designed the main block at Mill Hill to which the hospital went before World War I. (It is now in Northwood, but is still called Mount Vernon Hospital.) From 1914 until 1980 the Hampstead building became the National Institute for Medical Research. Among its directors living here were physiologist Sir Henry Dale, now commemorated with a blue plaque, and immunologist Sir Peter Medawar, of whom C P Snow said 'If he had designed the world, it would have been a better place'. Each of these directors shared a Nobel Prize for Medicine. From about 1980, the buildings were taken over by the National Institute for Biological Standards and Control, but within 10 years the site was being ripened for redevelopment. Included in the present luxury housing and apartments, jointly called Mount Vernon, is the 18th-century **Mount Vernon House** in the south-east corner.

We climb a slope to the left and find an attractive terrace of cottages, **Nos.1–6**, dating from 1800. Note the GH and coronet on the rainwater-head

of No.1, thanks to Sir Geoffrey Harmsworth, the press baron, who lived here in the 1930s. **Mount Vernon Cottages** date from about 1820, and the same period applies to **Abernethy House**, originally built as a parochial school for girls. This had become a lodging house by 1873, when Robert Louis Stevenson (see plaque) paid the first of several brief visits. His fellow lodger was (Sir) Sidney Colvin, then Slade Professor of Fine Art at Cambridge, who thought Hampstead would be a cure for the young writer's bad lungs, depression and drugs. Before leaving Mount Vernon, note the three old lamp posts, which are Listed, and the fire insurance plate on No.6, a reminder that up to about 1870, fire brigades were for subscribers only.

There are more 19th-century lamp posts round the corner in **HOLLY WALK** (for derivation see Holly Hill, p 25) and, on a clear day, there is a breathtaking view across the parish church to south London. On the west side is **Moreton**, a rough-cast house designed by Thomas Garner in 1896 (date on drainpipes) for art-lover Frederick Sidney, FSA. His initials and crest are over the delightful porch, and

7 Scenes in the North London Consumption Hospital (Mount Vernon Hospital), drawn by George Hutchinson c.1880.

his belief that 'God is Al in Al Thinges' is over the door.

Opposite is the splendid terrace called **HOLLY PLACE**, built in 1816. **No.8** was the home of actress Gwen Ffrangcon-Davies in the 1930s: she was first famous for partnering John Gielgud in *Romeo and Juliet* in 1924. **No.9** has a Hampstead plaque to show that this was the Watch House for the new police force from 1830. The barred cellar was probably used as cells. Since those days the Hampstead police have gone literally, but not rapidly, downhill. By 1834 they moved to the foot of Holly Hill, where the clock tower building now stands. By 1870 a new police station was opened on the west side of Rosslyn Hill, but in 1913 this was abandoned for the present site at the corner of Downshire Hill. **Nos.10&11**, which are technically in **HOLLYBERRY LANE**, are thought to have been connected with the old Watch House. No.10 may have been the sergeant's house and No.11 the stables. In the late 1930s, composer Sir William Walton (see plaque) was living in the former, and compositor Stanley Morison in the latter. Walton stayed here from 1935 to 1948, during which time he revised his famous *Façade* and wrote the film score for Laurence Olivier's *Henry V*. Morison was a typesetter only in the artistic sense, for in the 1930s, among other achievements, he redesigned *The Times* and transformed its *Literary Supplement*. He also used his genius in typography to expose the master-forger Thomas Wise (see p 22).

The centrepiece of Holly Place is **St Mary's Church**, begun in 1816. This is one of the earliest post-Reformation Roman Catholic churches in London, and takes its dedication from the old parish church before its rebuilding in 1747. The congregation grew around Abbé Morel, who settled in Hampstead in 1796, along with other refugees from the French Revolution; he died in 1852 and was buried in the porch. Two years previously the belfry façade was added, together with the Virgin and Child copied from an Argentinian statue. (The original church, being built before the Catholic Emancipation Act of 1829, had a discreetly plain front.) Inside is a portrait of Morel, painted by Clarkson Stanfield, and a Byzantine baldachino by Adrian Gilbert Scott. Among worshippers here during World War II was another notable French refugee, General de Gaulle (see also p 16). Among those married in this church have been Graham Greene in 1927 and (Dame) Judi Dench and Michael Williams in 1971: the Williamses have owned a house very near here for many years. **No.4** is now the presbytery (originally at No.8). **No.1** became St Vincent's Orphanage and School in 1872, but this closed in 1907 through lack of funds.

Lower down the hill are two culs-de-sac. **BENHAM'S PLACE** has nine terraced cottages, built in 1813 by William Benham, who was also a grocer and cheesemonger in the High Street. The road name does not appear in the Rate Books until 1829. The curious semi's of **PROSPECT PLACE**, stuccoed in front and weatherboarded behind, date from the 1790s and are painted delightfully in pink and pistacchio. There is a tradition that they were built by French refugee settlers, or even by Abbé Morel himself. Writer Paul Jennings lived at **No.4** in the 1950s, oddly briefly. The prospect over the churchyard extension is decidedly pleasing.

Return now to Holly Bush Hill and look across the green to where a group of tall Georgian houses (all Listed) marks the beginning of **WINDMILL HILL**. From left to right, **Volta House** and **Bolton House** were built in 1735, while **Windmill Hill House**, which now embraces its neighbour (formerly Enfield House), dates from 1730. An early-17th-century print shows the hill of Hampstead crowned with two windmills, and the sites have been noted in Holly Hill (p 26) and Hampstead Grove (p 30). The Victorian novelist and Hampstead lover Beatrice Harraden found this area 'as picturesque as old Blois itself and lived in by sweet presences'. Among the group of houses mentioned, the longest, if not sweetest, presence must have been that of Joanna Baillie, the Scottish literary lioness. She lived at Bolton House from 1791 until her death in 1851, and was one of the first women to be commemorated with an official plaque. Her *Plays on the Passions* may be forgotten now, but they caused a sensation in the 1790s, and in the following years her house was much visited by Byron, Wordsworth, Keats and especially Sir Walter Scott. As the latter said of her in *Marmion*, 'Avon's swans think Shakespeare lives again', so he gave her a scarf brooch and she knitted him a purse. In the 1930s, a rich artist called simply Gluck lived at Bolton House and had Sir Edward Maufe design her a studio, complete with minstrel's gallery, at the bottom of her garden: this is now **No.7** Windmill Hill. Charles Bean King built **Nos.1–6**, which have their dates 1894/5 under their eaves. Virginia Woolf was a frequent visitor to No.5 in Edwardian times, as she was taking Greek lessons there from the formidable feminist Janet Case. The student later recalled 'How I went hot and cold going to Windmill Hill'. The charming **Garden Cottage** is the old coach house of Fenton House (p 30), dating from the late 17th century (but altered).

Where the road ends at the Heath, some 100 metres further on, is the romantic 18th-century cottage **Capo di Monte**, previously called Upper Terrace Cottage or Siddons Cottage. In the absence of a plaque, an S-shaped wall plate recalls that the great actress Sarah Siddons stayed here in 1804–5. As with so many visitors, she came to Hampstead for her health, 'for the strong air and quiet surroundings', but particularly to be near a doctor who used the latest electrical cure for rheumatism. She doubtless also called on Joanna Baillie, in whose play *De Montfort* she had recently starred at Drury Lane. Her other great success was as Lady Macbeth, so much so that the play always *ended* with her sleep-walking scene. No wonder Mr Evans the draper in Hampstead High Street was so alarmed when she examined some material in his shop and demanded dramatically 'Will it wash?'.

In the 1940s Sir Kenneth Clark lived briefly in Capo di Monte, but he found the house too small: larger guests like Oliver Lyttelton filled the entire dining room, he complained in *The Other Half*. From 1949, this cottage orné was the home of the novelist, critic and broadcaster Marghanita Laski, who had a passion for lexicography: she was hailed as 'the undisputed queen of the English language'. When the Clark

family departed in 1943, they moved across the lane to **UPPER TERRACE** and found more elbow room in **Upper Terrace House**. This 18th-century mansion had been much altered in the 1930s, mainly by Oliver Hill, and Clark found the staircase 'hideous' until it proved solid enough to make an ideal air-raid shelter. After the war, when the house was overrun by his wife's fashion shows, he tended to work, he said, in a car parked in a cul-de-sac near Ken Wood. So they moved to Saltwood Castle in Kent. After Sir Kenneth came Sir Leon Bagrit, sometimes called 'the father of British automation'; he stayed in the house until 1976.

The street takes its name from the **terrace** of houses to the west, dating from about 1740, which has been variously divided up into two, three or four residences. For much of the 19th century this was the home of the philanthropic Jackson brothers, who built New Court, off Flask Walk (p 42) as model dwellings for workers. Hugh Jackson, a solicitor, also accommodated his father-in-law Sir William Beechey, the portrait painter, here; he died in Upper Terrace in 1839. Hugh's son Thomas became an architect who in 1883 redecorated the parish church chancel. Another remarkable resident here in the 1880s was Canon Alfred Ainger, Queen Victoria's chaplain and a local eccentric. He was a great friend of George du Maurier (p 29) and supplied him with ideas and captions for his cartoons – including the immortal *Curate's Egg*, published in *Punch* in 1895. Du Maurier's portrait of Ainger is now in the National Portrait Gallery. The house at the west end is **Upper Terrace Lodge** which, apart from having Florence Nightingale on its guest list, had the distinction of being redesigned in the 1880s by Basil Champneys and extended in the 1920s by Sir Edwin Lutyens. Curiously, the bricks at the front are now black. Next door, **No.5** is an award-winning avant-garde house by Rick Mather (also architect of ZENW3 in the High Street) built in 1997. The Victorian house on this site called The Priory was the home of sculptor John Foley, notable as the designer of the Albert Memorial's 'somewhat erotic' Asia group.

LOWER TERRACE is also named after a pretty row of late-Georgian houses, but of humbler stature. **No.2** was one of John Constable's homes in the summers of 1821 and 1822. Fig 8 shows the artist a few years later. He came to Hampstead mainly for his wife's health, for his letters show that he was anxious to get back to his big canvases in his Charlotte Street studio, but during his time in Lower Terrace he produced a large number of oil sketches of the area,

notably of the Heath and of Admiral's House. He also depicted the shed in his back garden and the family washing on the line. His painting of **No.4** (Fountain House) is in the V&A. **No.10**, Netley

8 John Constable c.1830 (portrait by an unknown artist).

Cottage, invisible behind its wall, dates back to 1779 and may have been a farm house. Additions were made by Ted Levy in 1983. The same architect designed the elephantine **Summit**

Lodge at the Whitestone Pond end of the road, but he died before this luxury development was completed in 1990. Among its twelve apartments, the Lodge claims to have the highest room in London (148 metres above sea level), but the whole complex is, as Pevsner remarks, 'far too prominent on its hilltop site'. The original house here was the Tudorised Hawthorne House, built in 1882 for W J Goode, the china merchant of South Audley Street. Its garden was on the site of what was once the Speakers' Corner of Hampstead and here, under a beech tree, Wesley and Whitefield and other famous orators preached.

A muddy lane to the south leads to **JUDGES' WALK**, which is not really a street, as it has no houses, but it is still remarkable for its name and its view. Variously called Prospect Walk, King's Bench Avenue and Upper Terrace Avenue, it became Judges' Walk early in the 20th century. The traditional reason for the name is that during the Great Plague of 1665 judges came here to hold the assizes. Historians who challenge this theory say that its name probably derives from nearby Branch Hill Lodge, once known as Judges' Bench House. Anyway, all agree that the view from here over Hendon and Harrow is spectacular. Constable has captured it in many of his paintings, though not all of them turn out to be quite accurate.

At the west end of Judges' Walk, steps lead down to **BRANCH HILL**, which was an old branch route to Child's Hill. Branch Hill also appears in many Constable views, especially its pond, seemingly varying in size from a horsepond to a miniature Buttermere. The pond dried up early in the 20th century, but its outline can still be seen near the junction with West Heath Road. Opposite the pond site, **The Chestnuts**, now a hotel, was for most of the 1930s the family home of the famous bass Paul Robeson. After his great success in *Show Boat*, especially with the song *Old Man River*, he was lionised in Hampstead by a distinguished crowd including his near neighbour Ramsay MacDonald (p 17).

To the north is the **Firecrest** development, on the site of Spedan Tower, a stately home (see also p 22) built by John Lewis, the store owner, whose middle name was Spedan; he died there in 1928, aged 93. Around **FIRECREST DRIVE** are 30 luxury flats in two 'domineering piles, eclectically detailed' (Pevsner) called **St Regis Heights** and **Savoy Court**.

To the south, **HEYSHAM LANE** leads to a famous development by Camden Council called **SPEDAN CLOSE**. The 42 semi's built in 1978 in the grounds of **Branch Hill Lodge** (see

below) were then called the most expensive Council houses ever built. Their foundations were largely the problem as the site, which was remote and on a steep slope, had particularly bad soil excavated from the Northern Line Underground at the start of the century. The average cost of the houses, ingeniously designed by Gordon Benson and Alan Forsyth (and others) was about £70,000. Building here was challenged as illegal by local conservation groups, who pointed out that Lord Glendyne had sold the land to the Council at a low price on condition that it be preserved as an open space.

The original Branch Hill Lodge was known in the early 18th century as Bleak Hall as well as Judges' Bench House. Since then the place had many associations with lawyers, notably Alexander Wedderburn, a crafty Lord Chancellor. Wedderburn, who became Earl of Rosslyn (see Rosslyn Hill, p 72), was known as 'the second Judge Jeffreys' for his harsh treatment of the Gordon Rioters. On his death, George III remarked 'He has not left a greater rogue behind in my dominions' – on hearing which Lord Thurlow said he was glad to know that the King was at least temporarily sane. The only other resident of note here was Lady Byron, who rented the house shortly after her separation from the poet. The present

house is partly by S S Teulon about 1868, but rebuilt in 1901 (this date is on it), becoming 'an Edwardian monster' according to Pevsner. It was bought by the Council from Lord Glendyne in 1965 and, complete with new wing, was turned into an old people's home. At the southern entrance is the Lodge's neo-Gothic **gatehouse**, bearing its date (1868) but, at present, no name. This was also designed by Teulon in the flamboyant style he used for St Stephen's, Rosslyn Hill. Thanks to the efforts of the Heath & Old Hampstead Society, the old kitchen garden below the gatehouse (now allotments) has been preserved for the public, and so has a nearby area of 'special nature conservation interest', known as Branch Hill Combe.

Across the road **Nos.1–5**, originally called Branch Hill Side, is a Victorian terrace with crow-stepped gables. Next comes **Branch Hill Mews** (a converted garage) and **Priory Cottage** (a converted coach house), followed by the modern **No.7** and the enticing 'Steps to Judges Walk'.

Route 3
The Wells
Between Flask Walk and East Heath Road

From Hampstead Tube station walk down the High Street and take the first left into pedestrianised Flask Walk; follow Flask Walk down the roadway which bends slightly to the right at the bottom into Well Walk. Continue to the fountainhead, past the Tavern.

I n 1698, six swampy acres around **WELL WALK**, 'being about certain medicinal waters', were given to the poor of Hampstead by the Gainsborough family, then

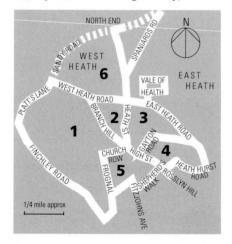

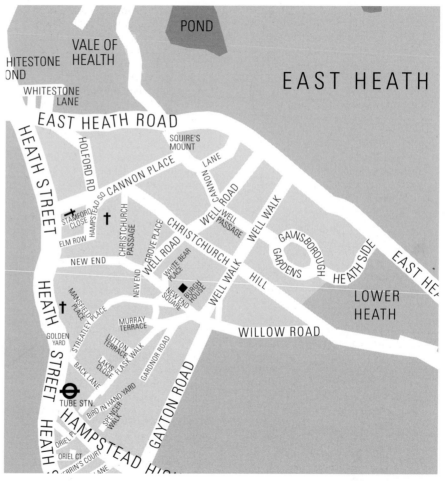

Lords of the Manor. The Wells Trust was formed, and an entrepreneur, John Duffield, was found to take a 21-year lease of the land to develop it into a spa. Opposite the present **drinking fountain** in Well Walk, an 1882 monument to the Gainsboroughs' gift, an 80-foot Long Room was quickly built, comprising a small Pump Room where the unpleasant chalybeate water (containing iron) was dutifully drunk, and a large Assembly Room where patients could recover and be entertained. Dancing, cards and concerts were organised. Between the Long Room and the tavern on the site of the present Wells Tavern (p 39) was a row of raffling booths. The story of the Spa and of the Wells Trust is fully told in *For the poor of Hampstead, for ever* (see Sources, p 96).

Unfortunately, Hampstead Wells became too popular with the wrong sort of people and, as early as 1709, their riotous assemblies were the subject of lawsuits by local residents. By 1721, the Spa had such a bad name that the lease was not renewed, and the Long Room rather surprisingly became a chapel-of-ease to the Parish Church. In the 1740s, when the church was being rebuilt, the whole congregation converged on the Well Walk chapel. With the building of Christ Church in 1852, the old Long Room again became vacant, but was soon filled by a Presbyterian congregation, until they built their chapel in 1862 in Willoughby Road. After some years as a Drill Hall for Hampstead Volunteers, it was finally demolished in 1882.

Retrace your steps across Christchurch Hill to the southern stretch of Well Walk and to the large block of Council flats labelled **Wells House**. A second Long Room and a Ball Room were built here in the 1730s, in an attempt to revive the Spa. These buildings were intended to be used more by residents than by visitors. Even so, Pope, Johnson and Mrs Thrale were among the distinguished visitors, as well as Fanny Burney, whose heroine in *Evelina* wrote about the horrors of an evening at Hampstead Wells. After the 18th century the second Spa buildings were turned into residences, but they were badly bombed in World War II and, despite much protest from preservationists, demolished in 1948. In their stead rose Wells House, the north-east wing being on the Long Room site. The architect C H James designed the blocks to harmonise with Burgh House (p 41), so much so that the Queen Anne house is nearly lost in their midst. Because of a post-war timber shortage, the roof had to be made of steel. The design won the RIBA's London Architecture Bronze Medal in 1949.

Across the road, **Nos.2–14 Well Walk** were built in 1880–2 by George Price, on the site of the Militia's drill-ground. They were given stepped gables to match the Militia buildings then in front of Burgh House (Fig 9). No.2 was the home in the 1970s of the artist Barbara Jones, author of the delightful *Follies and Grottoes*, and **No.12** was Max Beerbohm's temporary lodging in World War I. The plaque on **No.14** gives many claims to fame for Marie Stopes, the pioneer of birth control, but does not say when or why she came to this house, or that her marriage in 1911 to R R Gates was a disaster. She came in 1909, mainly to get away from her mother in Denning Road (p 53), and from her traumatic experiences in Well Walk she produced her best-selling book *Married Love*. The versatile actress Fay Compton lived in **No.22** in the early 1930s, having just successively played principal boy in panto, Ophelia to Godfrey Tearle's *Hamlet*, and the lead in Dodie Smith's *Autumn Crocus*. **No.26** was the last Hampstead home (1926–35) of Margaret Llewelyn Davies, champion of the Women's Cooperative Guild. She fought especially for the rights of married women 'tied to the washtub', and Leonard Woolf described her as 'a kind of Joan of Arc to her cohorts of housewives in her crusade against ignorance, poverty and injustice'. More recently, the house was occupied by the

Irons family, including in the 1970s and 1980s their film-star son Jeremy and his actress wife Sinead Cusack.

Past Christchurch Hill, **Nos.11–13** were built by C B King in 1879 and called The Limes. No.13 was the home of Poet Laureate John Masefield in 1914–16, but the blue plaque salutes H M Hyndman, who died here in 1921.

Hyndman was influential in the formative years of the Labour Party and has been called the 'classic top-hatted socialist'. **Nos.15–17** were also by C B King, in 1884. About the same time, **WELLS PASSAGE** was named and straightened from an old path linking the Spa's headspring with its fountain. The handsome **Manaton Lodge**, No.19, was

converted from the gardener's cottage in the grounds of Foley House and named after the owner's village in Devon. The building is Listed, as are **Nos.21–29**, also in the old Foley House garden. They were built by Henry Legg in 1882 for Edward Gotto of The Logs (see later); Gotto's initials are on the gateposts and on the wrought-ironwork linking the two blocks. The old name of this impressively decorated row, Foley Avenue, is still also visible. In the 1920s and 1930s Maxwell Garnett, son of William (p 21) and General Secretary of the League of Nations Union, lived at No.21, and in the early 1930s, just after the success of *The Good Companions*, J B Priestley had his first London home at No.27. The **seat** at the north end of Well Walk has replaced Keats's Seat, where this notable Hampstead resident was seen by antiquarian William Hone 'sitting and sobbing his dying breath into a handkerchief'.

Across the road, the elaborate **No.50**, originally Thwaitehead but now Klippan House, was built in 1881 by and for architect Ewan Christian: the date is on the wall and his initials on the weathervane. An inscription, now obliterated, round the cornice read 'God's Providence is my Inheritance' –

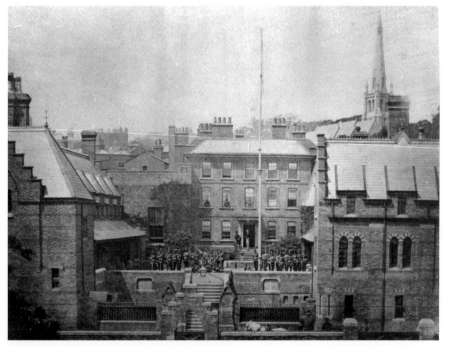

9 *Burgh House as HQ of the East Middlesex Militia, c.1870.*

which was particularly apt for this successful church architect; he was also co-architect of the National Portrait Gallery.

Going south, at the entrance to Gainsborough Gardens, **Wellside** has a tablet recording the site of the old Pump Room. In the 1960s this was the home of economist Lord Balogh, properly Baron Balogh of Hampstead. **No.46** Well Walk is early-18th-century, with delightful Gothic features added later. They must have pleased Temple Moore, another distinguished church architect, who lived here from 1892 to 1920. Among the first residents at **No.40** were the Constable family, as the blue plaque shows. On their arrival in 1827, the artist wrote ecstatically to his friend Fisher 'We are at length fixed in our comfortable little house in Well Walk....Our little drawing room commands a view unsurpassed in Europe'. Tragically his wife Maria died here the following year, but this remained his family home – he had seven children – until 1834. This was also the home before World War I of Charles Weekley, Poor Relief Officer of Hampstead, whose son had the misfortune to marry Frieda von Richthofen. It was at 40 Well Walk that Frieda dumped her two daughters in 1912 before eloping with D H Lawrence. Lovers of Sturge Moore's

poems and engravings will want to know that he lived here in the 1930s.

Nos.38&36 are also early-19th-century, with porches added later, but **Nos.34&32** are an early-18th-century pair. E V Knox (see also p 16) lived at No.34 from 1922 to 1945. Before World War I, the Socialist writer H N Brailsford lived at No.32. During that war it belonged to poets Dollie and Ernest Radford, and it was here that D H Lawrence and Frieda found refuge in 1917 after eviction from Cornwall as suspected spies. The visit is vividly described in Lawrence's *Kangaroo*. Film star Leslie Banks, also a notable Captain Hook on stage in *Peter Pan*, lived here in the 1930s and complained that the ghost of Keats used to turn on all his bath taps. The site of the postman's house where Keats lodged with his dying brother Tom is now under the **Wells Tavern**. This pub replaced The Green Man in 1850, which itself replaced a 'tavern with Dancing Room', dating back to the Spa period. The publican here in the 1920s was Sidney Strube, better known as a *Daily Express* cartoonist. Up until World War II, the Wells Hotel (its alternative name) was attracting 'long-stay thespians and colonials on three-month holidays'. The Tavern has always been owned by the Hampstead Wells Trust and is now their only building on the Wells Estate; it was

leased to Whitbreads from 1931 until recently. A colourful version of its history is displayed by its Well Walk entrance.

GAINSBOROUGH GARDENS covers the pleasure grounds of the first Spa, which included a bowling green to the north and an ornamental pond in the middle. The southern stretch was part of the garden of 46 Well Walk. The outline of the pond can be seen in the central **lawn**, which J B Priestley (p 38) and others used as a tennis court. In the northern shrubbery there is still an **ice house**, presumably a souvenir of the Long Room's catering department, but this is not viewable. What can be seen among the bushes is a **bell-turret**, salvaged from the demolished Trinity Church in Finchley Road. The Gardens were laid out by the Wells Trust in the 1880s, after its plan to run a road through the middle of them brought violent protest. A petition was launched to use the site for 'aged, infirm and poor artists and literary men', but this failed. The over-all planner and architect of about half the houses was Henry Legg: these include the gardener's **lodge**, dated 1886, and the elaborate **Nos.6–8**. The adjoining **Cottage on the Heath** was converted from the stables of No.6 in the mid-1930s. **Nos.11–14** were by Horace Field in the early 1890s. **Nos.3 and 4**, by E J May in 1883, were said to be the first modern houses with hot air heating.

Returning past the fountain, we climb up Wells Passage to **WELL ROAD**, which in Spa times led to the headspring and bath pond, on the site of **Nos.6–8**. These houses were built by C B King in 1881 and called Ivy Bank Villas. Early in the 20th century, three great pioneers lived here: No.6 was the home of (Sir) Ian MacAlister, the radical reformer of the Royal Institute of British Architects; No.7 housed the statistician Karl Pearson (see plaque); and in No.8 lived the Egyptologist Flinders Petrie, whose blue plaque went to his later home in Cannon Place (p 46).

No.5 was converted from a stable in 1894 by Horace Field. This was on the site of an Infant School (also used as a Drill Hall) dating back to the 1840s. **Nos.10–13** were erected by Allison & Foskett in 1880 and named Keats Villas. The author Richard Hughes lodged at No.10, just before publication of his *High Wind in Jamaica*. Both Nos.12 and 13 housed members of the Jay family (including Douglas and Peggy) for many years. **Nos.14&15** are among several architecturally surprising houses that have recently sprung up in Well Road in back gardens.

Nos.17–20 Well Road are in

The Logs, the name of which is as inexplicable as its style. Andrew Saint notes its 'wonderful uncertainty between Gothic and Italian', but Pevsner had no doubts about calling it 'a formidable atrocity' (Fig 10). The obscure architect responsible was J S Nightingale, who built it in 1868 for an even obscurer

civil engineer called Edward Gotto, who died here in 1897: his initials appear elaborately on the Cannon Lane side of the house. At some period a gateway labelled Lion House was added (did it come from the old zoo?). In 1951 the house was converted into maisonettes, one of which was occupied in the late

10   The Logs, Nos. 17–20 Well Road
(*J S Nightingale, 1868*).

1960s by pop-eyed comedian Marty Feldman, who much enjoyed, he said, this cockeyed house. Residents at **No.22**, Logs Cottage, in the 1950s were artist Vera Cuningham and her tenant Graham Reynolds, the art historian and authority on Constable. **Cannon Cottage** and **Providence Corner** date from the early 18th century. The former, once called Holly Hedge Cottage, was the home of Daphne du Maurier and her husband in the 1930s. In the southern stretch of Well Road, **Weatherall Lodge** is bigger than it looks; it was probably converted from the 18th-century stables of a Spa building. **No.1 Wellmount Studios** bears a plaque to Mark Gertler, who painted here in 1932/33, although he spent many more years in Rudall Crescent (p 53).

Behind the studios is **GROVE PLACE**, of which **Nos.29–31** were cleverly converted from the Bickersteth Hall in 1970. Topped by a couple of cupolas, the hall was built for Christ Church in 1895 and named after its famous vicar, who became Bishop of Exeter. Confusingly, an 1871 St Pancras plaque and an 1886 Jubilee plaque, attributed to Mrs Edward Gotto, have been added to the building. Across the road are 28 'model dwellings for artisans', or **Grove Place Flats**, built about 1914 on the site of the Spa's Bath House by the local Baptist benefactor

Herbert Marnham (see p 17).

At the southern end of Well Road is the pub Ye Olde White Bear (p 45) and behind it is **WHITE BEAR PLACE**. Adjoining it is the non-rectangular **NEW END SQUARE**. This was developed during the Spa period, the grander **Nos.16–20** being early-18th-century and the lesser houses a little later. The entrance to No.20 is wisterically pretty. Nearly all the Square's houses had to be rebuilt or replaced after bombing in World War II (Fig 11). **Nos.7–17** and **22–26** became Council flats. **No.36**, once known as Lion Works, has housed job masters, motor engineers and various antiques enterprises. **No.40**, with the Tuscan portico, was built in 1759 as the Hawk Tavern and rebuilt in 1815 after a fire. It had become the highly respectable Rose Lodge when Alfred, Lord Tennyson installed his mother here in the 1860s, and it was linked by a hole in the wall with 75 Flask Walk, where his sister lived. From 1932, No.40 was the home of artists Daphne and George Charlton (samples of their work are in Burgh House). Stanley Spencer was a frequent visitor here during World War II, and his portrait of his close friend Mrs Charlton is in the Tate.

Across the road is **Burgh House**, which was lucky to survive all the bombing. Built in 1703, it soon became the residence of the Spa physician,

William Gibbons: his initials are on the ornate wrought-iron gates. The Revd Allatson Burgh, who lived here until his death in 1856, was an unpopular vicar of St Lawrence Jewry in the City, but he should be remembered locally as one of the protesters in 1829 who helped prevent the Lord of the Manor from building on the Heath. From 1858 to about 1881, Burgh House was the Officers' Mess of the Royal East Middlesex Militia (Fig 9, p 38), with barracks in Willow Road. Later residents included Thomas Grylls, of the famous stained-glass painters Burlison and Grylls; Dr George Williamson, art expert extraordinary and adviser of Pierpont Morgan among others; and Elsie Bambridge, daughter of Rudyard Kipling. After World War II, the house was bought by the local Council, which from 1979 leased it to the Burgh House Trust, who run it as a community and arts centre, which includes a café (the Buttery), an art gallery and the Hampstead Museum of local history.

At the corner of New End Square with **FLASK WALK**, sporting a dignified Doric portico, is Rose Mount, **No.75**, dating from 1812. Captain Richard Jesse, RN, who lived here in the 1860s, married Tennyson's sister Emily, and nobly accommodated his mother-in-law in the adjoining house (see above). The studded **door** in the wall opposite used to be the Debtors' Entrance to the infamous Newgate Gaol. It was bought by the owner of Gardnor House (see below), Major Paget, when the gaol was demolished in 1902. Note the brickwork

Hampstead's first recorded fair. More permanently on the green were village stocks and the Watchman's hut, complete with two overnight cells. All we have now is the **Baths** building

11 New End Square during World War II, with blast shelter (centre) and Emergency Water Supply (left).

above in the shape of a Beadle's hat. **No.73**, formerly Catherine Cottage, now has its own plaque reading 'Flask House, built 1734'. Along the street is the nucleus of another village **green**, which was large enough in 1712 to hold Happy

(Listed), designed by Henry Legg for the Wells and Campden Charity, but in 1981 converted into town houses (one called The Washhouse). There are two sorts of **Flask Cottages** nearby – old ones with twisted chimneys, and the 1950s variety ingeniously devised by a Council architect. Next door is **Boade's Mews**, both a passage and a house, converted from a garage belonging

(surprisingly) to High Close in Holford Road; Boade's Corner was the old name for this area.

Here also is **MURRAY TERRACE**, a name first found in the 1840 Rate Book, possibly derived from William Murray, Earl of Mansfield, who had many local connections, including Ken Wood. On the other side of Flask Walk, **GARDNOR ROAD** was developed in 1871/2 ('with impoverished inspiration' comments Alastair Service) in the grounds of **Gardnor House**. The names come from Thomas Gardnor, whose family owned a large slice of central Hampstead, and who built the house about 1736. There is a grand Gardnor tomb in the parish churchyard, near the main gate. Other residents in the house have included local historian G W Potter and, in the 1980s, writers Kingsley Amis and Elizabeth Jane Howard. The house is now Listed II★.

Back in Flask Walk, the pleasant terrace **Nos.53–67** was another built by Thomas Gardnor, in 1811. The Hampstead Subscription Library started at No.65 in 1833, with Constable among the founder-members. To the south is **LUTTON TERRACE**, an alley seen on the 1814 map. Lutton is a common English place-name, but has no obvious local association. At the end of the alley is **New Court**, two blocks of forty 'model dwellings' erected by the philanthropic Jackson brothers of Upper Terrace (p 33). The old name, New Buildings, can be seen on a faded sign. The main block was built in 1855 and the smaller one, with a reading room, in 1871. A war memorial stone shows that fifty residents went off to World War I, 'of whom ten died for the good cause'. From the 1960s there have been plans to demolish and redevelop these blocks and many flats were squatted, notably by pop stars the Sex Pistols and Boy George. The buildings are now Listed and owned by Camden Council. Despite short leases they appear to hold a thriving community.

Most of **Nos.35–41** Flask Walk are early-19th-century workers' cottages, and so is **No.48** across the road, part of which was for many years a grocer's shop. (Legend had it that Dr Crippen bought his Hovis loaves there.) **LAKIS CLOSE** was designed in 1973 by Gerson Rottenberg for a Greek Cypriot developer, who named it after his son (Lakis, pronounced 'lackeys', is short for Michael). Also modern and meritorious are **Nos.30–36** Flask Walk, replacing the Salvation Army barracks and a Montessori school.

The Flask is a Listed pub, though this version dates only from 1874. The original Lower Flask Tavern, which gave this old street its name, was the place where Spa water was once bottled for sale in the City. The water could be bought in Fleet Street at threepence a flask, and customers were earnestly advised to beware of imitations. In Samuel Richardson's 1748 novel *Clarissa*, the Lower Flask was described as 'a place where second-rate persons are to be found occasionally in a swinish condition'. Much has changed since then, including the pub sign, which now pictures the wrong sort of flask. At the High Street entrance to Flask Walk there used to be a two-storey superstructure like the one over Perrin's Court nearly opposite; this fell down in 1911. In 1973 the Council created a pedestrian-preferred **precinct** here (though cars can still intrude), and won a Civic Trust Award for it. Of the old shops, **Nos.1–7** are basically early-18th-century, and **Nos.2&4** early-19th-century.

Heading north off Flask Walk and backing the High Street is **BACK LANE**. This was called Garden Place on the 1862 map, and part of it was Alfred Terrace in the 1888 Directory, probably after Lord Alfred Paget, who owned land here. As in Flask Walk, many of the workers' cottages have been taken over and beautified by brainworkers. **Radius Works**, once a jobmaster's stables, has been happily converted to offices. Down a minute alley next door are **Keil's Cottages**, which once connected with Mr Keil, a baker in the High Street

(on the Tube station site). More offices have appeared higher up the road in a backwater at **No.5A**, once called Alfred Terrace Mews.

At the top of Back Lane, the straitened **STREATLEY PLACE** wanders off towards New End. Called Brewers Lane in the 18th century and Brewhouse Lane in the 19th, the present 'deliberately neutral' name was chosen in the 1890s to improve its image, according to the GLC Street Naming Section. **Streatley Flats** were built in the early 1900s by the benevolent Herbert Marnham (p 17). There is a myth that **MANSFIELD PLACE** was built for the police, with constables in the cottages and the sergeant-in-charge in the house at the end. Equally unsupported is the theory that these houses were designed for dairy workers, with the head dairyman in the larger house. More certain is it that this now charming enclave was developed on Campbell's Nursery Garden in 1860/1.

Back in Streatley Place, the date of **New End Primary School**, 1906, is clearly seen. The building of the school was encouraged by the Education Act of 1903, and the LCC architect was T J Bailey. Like UCS in Frognal (p 14), this is a school with a river running through its foundations, in this case part of the Fleet. A new **nursery school** has just been built in Streatley Place, as part of the New End Hospital development (below). At the corner with New End (Fig 12), the schoolkeeper's house was once a beer shop called The City Arms.

The name **NEW END** appears in

12 New End, by J P Emslie 1880. The pole in front of W Taylor's shop once carried the inn sign The City Arms.

the local burial register for 1696, so some of this development pre-dates the Spa. The 'end' here means outer district, like Hampstead's North, South and West Ends, which shows that the original colony of cottages was on the outskirts of the village. None of the cottages has survived, but **No.30** is Listed as early-18th-century, with flush-framed windows. (After 1715 all window frames had to be recessed from the wall face, as a fire precaution.)

Nearly all the houses in the lower stretch of New End started in some sort of trade, which explains their wide windows. The 1899 Directory shows a dairy, a baker, a chimney sweep, a farrier and at **No.57** a fried fish shop. Over this corner shop can be seen the name Southwell Terrace, which applied to this side of the street only. On the building opposite, **No.16**, Heathside School, is a plaque commemorating the dispensary and soup kitchen erected here in 1853, by voluntary contributions. This was done as a thank-offering for the sparing of the parish from the 'noisome pestilence', a cholera plague. The architect was R Hesketh and the chief instigator was Hampstead's vigorous vicar, Thomas Ainger. This Provident Dispensary, which offered cheap medicine to the poor, and a pint of soup for a penny, was made redundant in the 1940s and converted into an architect's office in 1955, at which time the plaque was salvaged from the waiting-room.

Nos.10–14, which are Listed as a group, date from 1725. Higher up the hill, much of the new luxury development (**Kendall's Hall**, **Young's Court**, and **Upper Hampstead Walk**) is based on the old Hampstead Workhouse, dating back to about 1850. Kendall and Young were among the architects involved. The workhouse became New End Hospital in World War I and its **water tower** and innovative **circular wards block** (architect, Charles Bell) have been preserved; these, along with the boilerhouse **chimney**, have now been

Listed. The hospital, which was eventually annexed by the Royal Free, was closed in 1985.

Across the road, the **Duke of Hamilton** is the latest version of an alehouse mentioned in the Manor Survey of 1762. The cobbled alley at the side once led to the stables. The building next door began life as a mortuary in 1890, but has been the **New End Theatre** from 1974. A number of productions and managements have died since then – but the shows go happily on. Various play publicists have claimed that Karl Marx's body was laid out in this mortuary, and even that Keats watched post-mortems here. (They died in 1883 and 1821 respectively.) Further downhill are the Council flats **Carnegie House** (architects A and J Soutar), named after Hampstead's first woman Mayor, wife of the vicar of the parish church, and opened by her in 1948. **Ye Olde White Bear** used to show its 1704 foundation stone, but it has been much rebuilt since then. The open space towards Christchurch Hill was once known as White Bear Green.

CHRISTCHURCH HILL is shown as Green Man Lane on the 1862 map, named after a pub on the site of the Wells Tavern. A few years later – perhaps to improve its image – it was rechristened by the newly built church at the top of the hill, which is actually in Hampstead Square. At the corner with Well Road, **Acrise Cottage** has a Kentish name; it was converted from an old stable belonging to the second Spa, with a china cupboard made from a hay-chute. Towards the north, **No.55** was the last home of popular novelist Pamela Frankau, who died here in 1967. Most of **Nos.57–59**, Christchurch Place, were built by Herbert Marnham as workers' flats, at the same time as their neighbours in Grove Place (p 41). The northernmost block is, however, dated 1903. At the top of the hill, the pleasantly villagey **Christchurch School**, designed in Tudor style by W and E Habershon, dates from 1855. Note its attractive chimneys and railings. Behind here, **CHRISTCHURCH PASSAGE** follows an old path seen on the 1746 map. It was called West View Lane in the mid-19th century, and led to the Ebenezer Strict Baptist Chapel, used by a splinter group from the Holly Mount congregation.

On the other side of Christchurch Hill, below Well Road, the charming **No.26**, long known as Sunnybank, dates from the early 19th century, but has been much altered and extended. **Nos.16–22** display their dates, 1877–78, and a crested K, which means they were built by Charles Bean King of Church Row. The author Ivor Brown and his wife Irene Hentschel, respected drama critic and drama director respectively, lived at No.20 for half a century. Her father was Carl Hentschel, the original of Harris in *Three Men in a Boat*. On the lower slopes of Christchurch Hill, **Nos.1–41** were built about 1865 and numbered in reverse order (until 1937). The Trustees of the Wells Estate across the road thought at the time that the houses were 'of a very inferior class'. Several have sold recently for about £1 million each.

We retrace our steps via Well Road to **CANNON LANE**, which is bristling with late-18th-century cannon bollards and early-19th-century lamp posts; they are all Listed. Behind the ancient wall on the left, the garden of Cannon Hall has been growing houses, so the door to the old **lock-up** is not what it used to be: it is now the entrance to **No.11**, complete with entryphone. The Hampstead plaque explains that the lock-up was used from about 1730 to 1830, when business was transferred to Holly Walk (p 31). Daphne du Maurier, who grew up in Cannon Hall (p 46), described in *Growing Pains* the game she played in this cell, 'its blackened walls and barred slit windows daunting to whichever of us was taking the part of the prisoner at the time'.

At the top of the Hill, **SQUIRE'S MOUNT** took its name from Joshua Squire, who built the fine residence of that name in 1714. The house has since been divided, one part being called **Chestnut Lodge**, with a neo-Georgian addition by Horace Field. The family of Edwin Field, the law reformer, lived in the main house for many years and left it to the National Trust. Edwin died in 1871, after rescuing a man from the Thames. In the late 1930s this was the home of Clive Brook, star of silent films (eg *Christine of the Hungry Heart*) and talkies (eg *Cavalcade*). The charming terrace of cottages **Nos.1–5** is labelled 'Squires Mount Croft 1704', but this is misleading. The terrace is basically mid-19th-century and the date tablet is thought to have wandered in from a house at the rear, visible on the 1746 map. **Nos.11&12** have an early Victorian look, but were built in the 1950s. Actor Richard Burton was an early inhabitant, soon joined by Elizabeth Taylor and family. Composer Sandy Wilson (see Denning Road, p 53) later lived at No.12.

CANNON PLACE sports hefty cannon bollards as well as the stately **Cannon Hall**, dating from about 1720 but much altered. The cannon (objects and name) were contributed by Sir James Cosmo Melville, Secretary to the East India Company, who lived at the Hall from 1838. Part of the outbuilding with the cupola was once a magistrates' court, which dealt with the prisoners in the above-mentioned lock-up. Sir Gerald du Maurier, who lived here

from 1916 until his death in 1934, used the room for billiards. Sir Gerald (see plaque) was the first Captain Hook in *Peter Pan* (1904) and one of the last great actor-managers. He was the son of George du Maurier (p 29) and father of Daphne. Next door No.12, the delightful **Cannon Lodge**, is also early-18th-century, with fishtail tile-hanging. This was the parsonage of Christ Church before the present vicarage was built as **No.10** in 1907.

The houses on the north side, **Nos.7–25**, were built in the grounds of old Heathfield House by William Shepherd in 1875–77; they were originally called Heathfield Gardens. In the 1880s poet W J Cory (see Pilgrim's Lane, p 54) was living at No.25 and at about the same time the composer (Sir Henry) Walford Davies was at No.15. He was organist at Christ Church in the 1890s and during this time redesigned the organ. The blue plaque on **No.5** shows that Sir Flinders Petrie, a pioneer of systematic archaeology, lived here from 1919 to 1935, when not actually digging up Egypt. **No.1**, which shows its date, 1879, is one of many local studio houses by Batterbury and Huxley.

At the entrance to **HAMPSTEAD SQUARE** is **Christ Church**, which was built in 1852 by the rich congregation of Well Walk Chapel (p 37). The architect was Samuel

Daukes, noted for his railway stations and for Colney Hatch Lunatic Asylum (the centrepiece of Friern Park Hospital). Pevsner calls the style 'correct but dull ecclesiological Middle Pointed'. In the 1860s, the great George Gilbert Scott, living in Admiral's House, became consulting architect and added a west gallery, but this was later removed. In the 1870s his eponymous son supervised repairs to the spire, a great local landmark, and added the west porch. Ewan Christian (see above) designed the north aisle. Records show that on one Sunday in 1886, 2325 people attended this church; the comparable figure in 1902/3 was 909. The coming of Christ Church turned Hampstead Square into a polygon. The 1762 map shows a rectangular grove here, called The Square. This open space was used in the early 19th century by strolling players and later by the Victoria Tea Gardens.

There are several houses of age and beauty here. **Nos.1&2** date from about 1720. **Nos.7–9**, a terrace of about 1730, bears a memorial to Newman Hall, a once-famous Congregational minister and hymn-writer, whose widow adapted two houses into homes for the aged. Newman Hall died in 1902 at **No.6**, an early-18th-century house called Vine House and still having a vine in view. **No.11** was the last home of the Rev John

Llewelyn Davies (1826–1916), father of Margaret (see Well Walk, p 37) and, like her, a great champion of women's rights. He supported so many unfashionable causes that he was transferred from St Marylebone to distant Kirkby Lonsdale, but he was finally appointed Chaplain to George V. **No.12**, Lawn House, is very early 18th-century, with flush-framed windows and later extensions. The poet and mystic Evelyn Underhill lived here in the 1930s and died here in 1941; she is buried in the parish churchyard. She was a disciple of Baron von Hügel (see below), a collaborator of Tagore and revered by T S Eliot. She has been called a 'very human, very English saint'.

The terrace next door, **Nos.10–14**, is in **ELM ROW** and was built in the 18th century over the stables of the 'Duke of Hamilton' in New End. The grander terrace, **Nos.1,3&5**, dates from about 1720, but was mostly re-faced in the late 19th century by local builder C B King: the *fleur de lys* on the front are his marks (cf. Church Row, p 78). No.3 has a Hampstead plaque to Sir Henry Cole, who lived here in 1879–80. Apart from being largely responsible for founding the Victoria and Albert Museum, where a Henry Cole Wing has been opened, he is said to have originated the custom of sending Christmas cards. In 1923 D H Lawrence stayed some months at No.1,

in the room with the verandah, and used the area as background for his story *The Last Laugh*. **No.1** is Listed II★, as is Elm Lodge, **No.2**, which was built about 1732 and used to face New End: this may explain its present blank look, with more windows bricked up than glazed. The flights of steps were added about 1930, when the house was split up. There was a row of elms down this street in the 18th century.

Round the corner between 114 and 116 Heath Street is the entrance to **STAMFORD CLOSE**, a nearly secret passage leading to Hampstead Square; it is visible on the 1762 map. In the 1930s, when six old cottages here were condemned, the Close was said to be 'a miserable dark square – a black spot'. Its name derives from nearby Stamford Lodge (now demolished), where in 1823 Constable and his family were among the lodgers.

Between Hampstead Square and East Heath Road is **HOLFORD ROAD**, which takes its name from a worthy Hampstead family of the 19th century; the Holfords were involved in the Parish School, the Literary and Scientific Society, the Rifle Volunteers *et al.* (For their history see *Camden History Review* 6.) They lived in a mansion round the corner in East Heath Road. The blue plaque on **No.4** salutes the theologian Friedrich von Hügel, Baron

of the Holy Roman Empire, who lived here from 1892 to 1903. Among many local good deeds he helped to rescue St Mary's, Holly Place, from closure around 1900. **No.4b** was the home in the 1960s of Jane Lane, the prolific historical novelist. Halas and Batchelor, makers of cartoon films such as *Animal Farm*, lived at **No.6** for many years. The towering **High Close** was built by W H Murray in 1884; it soon became a guest house and, until recently, an old people's home.

At the top of East Heath Road, near Whitestone Pond, is **WHITESTONE LANE**, which leads to a handsome huddle of houses. Of these **Gangmoor**, which is early-18th-century, was briefly the home of George du Maurier and family in the 1860s. 'A more genial home', he wrote, 'could not be found anywhere'. **Whitestone House**, once called The Lawn, is of Regency origin, but was much enlarged by Clough Williams Ellis in 1934. Under the lawn were found foundations of a studio, presumably used by the artist Mark Anthony, who died here in 1886, and possibly by Constable, who rented the adjoining Albion Cottage in 1820. Sir Herbert Barker, the controversial bone-setter or, rather, 'manipulative surgeon', lived at The Lawn from 1912. He was the champion of 'unqualified practitioners', whose gift of healing reputedly saved over 30,000 patients from needing operations or appliances. **The Cottage** was rebuilt in 1908 for the widow of Sir Joseph Duveen (see Spaniards Road, p 87). In 1933–5 the champion boxer Jimmy Wilde lived here and renamed it, for obvious reasons, Lonsdale; he was often seen at the gymnasium at 64 Heath Street. On the pavement nearby is a bewildering **bollard**, marked 'Sommers Town 1817', which has strayed in from another part of Camden.

Once known as Middle Heath Road, **EAST HEATH ROAD** was finally so named in the 1860s. A century later it was threatened with plans to turn it into the Hampstead Village By-Pass, but the dreaded six-lane motorway was averted by the efforts of local protesters, headed by the Heath and Old Hampstead Society. At the top of the hill, **Bellmoor** flats are named after the imposing residence on this site of Thomas Barratt, author of the monumental *Annals of Hampstead*, who lived there 1877–1914 (Fig 12). Barratt made his money from Pears' Soap, whose image he boosted with the *Bubbles* advertisement and *Pears Cyclopaedia*. Apart from a brown plaque to Barratt, the flats bear a note of their height above sea-level (435$\frac{1}{2}$ ft) and above the cross of St Paul's (16$\frac{1}{2}$ ft). Among early flat-dwellers here in the 1930s were Wimbledon champion Bunny Austin and conductor Sir Thomas Beecham.

No.22 East Heath Road, Ladywell Court, is the remains of a mansion that was the home of the Holford family. The house was known as Heathfield in the 1870s, when the grounds were sold for building and the Hampstead Reformatory School for girls moved here from Church Row. Its present healthy name came with its use as a nursing home from before World War I. The whole building was reconditioned in the 1950s.

Lower down the hill, below Squire's Mount, is **No.17**, which bears a blue plaque to the writer Katherine Mansfield and her husband Middleton Murry. They moved here soon after their marriage in 1918. The house was then called 2 Portland Villas but, as it was tall and grey, they called it The Elephant. Their residence here attracted a large number of leading literati. On one day, according to the Mansfield diaries, she entertained Lytton Strachey, the Huxleys and the Woolfs. In the autumn of 1920, when Hampstead air had failed to cure her consumption, she moved to Italy.

Nos.14&15 are two charming cottages, built in 1770 and traditionally once used by Heath shepherds; the property now belongs to the National Trust. **Foley House** was thought to be the residence built for himself in 1698 by Duffield, the first Spa manager, at the then high cost of £1000. But the latest DCMS List suggests a date of about 1771. Apparently named after a Captain Foley who lived here in 1805–8, the house was leased in the 1880s to Edward Gotto of The Logs (see Well Road). It was he who added the porch and developed part of the grounds. The old stables are included in the current Listing. In 1990 the house was bought from the Wells and Campden Trust by a pop-group drummer for £2$\frac{1}{2}$ million.

The blocks of flats on the north side, **The Pryors**, were allowed on the Heath because there had been a house on this site for many years. This belonged to Thomas Pryor, a rich brewer, who married one of the Hoares of Hampstead in 1802. Some years before demolition in 1902, the house was occupied by landscape artist Walter Field, son of Edwin of Squire's Mount; a splendid example of his work is in the Burgh House music room. The flats, designed in Edwardian baroque by Hall and Waterhouse, have accommodated a number of literary gents, notably novelist Ernest Raymond, author of *We*, *The Accused* and many other absorbing tales. As a change from all the Captain Hooks who populate these pages, the Pryors can boast a famous Peter Pan – Jean Forbes Robertson, who lived here with her husband André van Gyseghem from the 1930s.

Opposite the flats, **No.8** was built by Ewan Christian at the same time, and with the same chimneys, as his 50 Well Walk (p 38). Controversial philosopher Cyril Joad lived for many years at **No.4**, which he found 'ugly but comfortable'. Acclaimed for his performance on the BBC's Brains Trust, he also won local fame in the 1930s for championing mixed hockey on the Heath, which had been forbidden until then; he died in 1953 and was buried in the parish churchyard. Kingsley Martin, editor of *The New Statesman*, shared this house with him during World War II.

The creeper-covered **East Heath Lodge** and the semi-detached **South Lodge**, which is in **HEATH SIDE**, were built about 1784. The former was the home of Sir Arthur Bliss (see plaque) in the 1930s; the latter has its original doorcase with Tower-of-the-Winds capitals (see Athens, but not in this book). Both have handsome railings with double-axe gateposts. **Nos.1&2** Heathside are a delightful pair of bow-fronted cottages dating from 1805, says the DOE List but possibly 1775, according to the latest DCMS List because of the iron balcony by James Wyatt.

13   Thomas Barratt in his Landseer library at Bellmoor, 1904.

49

Route 4
The Late Developers
Between Gayton Road and South End Road

We begin at the bottom of **WILLOW ROAD,** which borders the Heath and climbs from Downshire Hill to Well Walk. The area is shown in a Chatelaine engraving of 1752, and it includes a wide track leading up to the second Long Room in Well Walk. The willows arrived in 1845, when Sir Thomas Maryon Wilson planted a great many trees on the Heath despite – or possibly

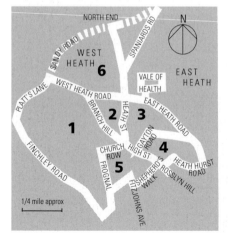

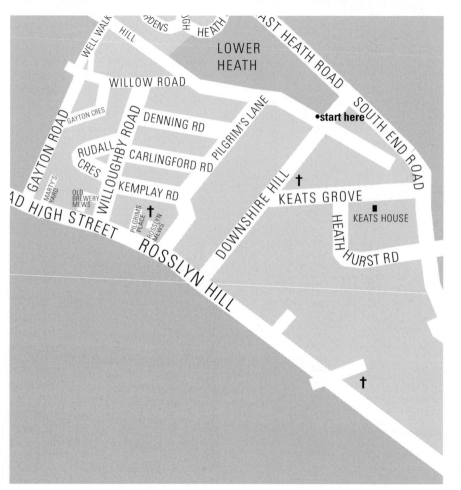

because of – the protests of his copyholders. The original track ran beside a branch of the Fleet River, which rose on the New End School site. By 1829, the riverbed in Willow Road had become a popular dumping ground and was described as 'an exposed sewer', which may have discouraged earlier development, but certainly encouraged fine beds of watercress. Most of the present houses in the street were built about 1880.

In 1938 the modern terrace, **Nos.1–3**, replaced an 18th-century row of cottages (Fig 14) with what the Hungarian architect, Ernö Goldfinger, called 'an adaptation of 18th-century style'. His design brought much protest from local preservationists – and from author Ian Fleming, who named one of his *James Bond* villains after the architect. But the project had strong support from architectural pundits. 'The terrace' wrote Pevsner 'goes infinitely better with the Georgian past of Hampstead than anything Victorian.' **No.2** was bought by the National Trust in 1994, its first modernist house, and is now Listed II★ and open to the public. **Nos.12–14** are an ornate trio showing their date, 1879. In Edwardian times **No.22** was the home of Roger Fry, pioneer of Post-

14 Lower Heath Cottages, c.1906, replaced in 1938 by Nos.1–3 Willow Road .

Impressionism and, in the 1920s, **No.26** housed not only Alfred Bacharach, prodigious scientist and musician, but (Professor) Cyril Joad. The attractive **Nos.33–41**, labelled **Willow Cottage's** (sic), were built about 1857 on the site of some almshouses; traditionally, the new cottages were to house watercress pickers. No.40 achieved fame in the 1970s when its occupants, Lawrence and Pat Hutchins, wrote a story about it for *Jackanory*, namely *The House that Sailed Away*, which was later published. The old shop front of **No.49** now shows pottery, instead of the grocery it offered for years.

On the other side of the road, opposite Gayton Crescent, **Willow Hall**, formerly Willow Buildings, and also known as Toad Hall, began life in 1863 as Militia Barracks (see Burgh House, p 41). They were built as married quarters for sergeants and bandsmen, and the design was probably based on Prince Albert's model dwellings, shown at the Great Exhibition in 1851. By 1964 they were in a far from model condition and an 8-year battle began for their improvement led by long-term resident Tony Clarke, now Baron Clarke of Hampstead. The property now belongs to Camden

Council. Secretly living here in 1966 was the spy George Blake, en route from Wormwood Scrubs to Moscow. Notable residents at **Nos.50–54** have included musician Hans Keller and architect Charles Rennie Mackintosh.

In the middle of the 19th century, a large paddock at the north-west end of Willow Road was divided into about 40 allotments. By 1870 these had been redeveloped into **GAYTON ROAD** and **CRESCENT**. The owner of this 4-acre site was barrister George Nathan Best, of Bayfield Hall in Norfolk, and the fact that there is a village called Gayton (meaning goat farm) not far away has suggested this as the origin of the street name. There is also the theory that one of the Potter family, who built the houses here, had Gayton as a second name, but history does not relate which was christened first, the street or the Potter. The whole area was brightened in the 1970s by the formation of the Gayton Residents' Association, aimed at fighting rat runs and pavement parkers and other environmental pests, and responsible for Hampstead's first series of street festivals.

Among distinguished residents in Gayton Crescent in the 1970s were author John Le Carré at **No.1**, and film director Karel Reisz at **No.8**. Novelist John Braine came to **No.4A** from New End and died here in 1986. The modern terrace **Nos.18–22** was built, with **Nos.36–38** in Gayton Road, on the Gayton Nursery Garden site in 1970. The architects were Ted Levy, Benjamin and Partners, so adept at squeezing attractive pints into half-pint plots. From the first, the original no-nonsense houses in Gayton Road attracted a good mix of professional classes and workers, with a preponderance of dressmakers. In the 1880s, **No.10** was the Hampstead High School for Girls 'under Influential Patronage'. Around 1908, **No.9** was the home of essayist Robert Lynd and, in the 1970s, of another literary lion, Melvyn Bragg. (The road featured in his 1971 novel *The Nerve* as Tagon Street.) **No.61**, the OXFAM shop, has previously been an ironmonger's, a dairy and a betting shop: one of the dairyman's daughters is said to have been Ethel Le Neve, friend of Dr Crippen. Opposite, **Vine Cottage** is on the site of two small tenements belonging in 1830 to a tailor at 23 High Street. The present bungalow was built in 1902/3. The actor Wilfrid Hyde-White lived here in the 1930s. After World War II, part of the land was transferred to Crowe's, the funeral furnishers, in the High Street, and their lease stated that they must not disturb the amenities of the cottage by transporting coffins near it. The property's vine has been known to produce over a 100 lb of grapes.

Between Gayton Road and Downshire Hill, the large Carlile House and its grounds were sold to the British Land Company for building in 1875. The resultant streets are full of Victorian middle-class town houses and terraces, complete with attics for skivvies. **WILLOUGHBY ROAD**, which followed part of the drive of Carlile House, was named after the Willoughby family who actually sold the estate. Benjamin Willoughby, a solicitor, had married Edward Carlile's daughter. His second son, incidentally, became Mayor of Holborn and also had a street named after him there. At the High Street end, **Trinity Close** was converted in the 1970s from the hall of the Trinity Presbyterian Church, erected in 1862 (before the road was built) and demolished a century later. **Willoughby Hall School** next door, with two foundation stones – one saying 'We will do thee good' – was built as a YMCA in 1886. After many years of varied use, notably as the Hampstead Spiritual Temple and an Air Training Corps base, the hall became a school in 1989.

Another hall opposite, **Rosslyn Hall**, has a longer history. 'A Meeting Place for Protestant Dissenters' was registered in 1691 at Carlile House, then the home of Isaac Honeywood, but when the congregation grew,

Honeywood built a chapel next to his stables on this site. This was rebuilt in 1828, and much of Rosslyn Hall's present structure dates from this time. But by 1862 it again proved too small and the present chapel on Rosslyn Hill (see below) was built nearby; the hall was then used mainly as a school and dancing academy.

No.14 was the home of Don Salvador de Madariaga in 1916-21, a scholarly Anglo-Spanish writer of great style. The recently rebuilt No.26 shows its original date and the initials of its first owner, C J Coates. Christopher Coates not only ran a China and Glass Warehouse in the High Street, but was Registrar of Marriages and Collector of the Poor Rate. In 1852 his lodger in his High Street house (now demolished) was the struggling artist Ford Madox Brown (see p 28). D H Lawrence and his wife Frieda had rooms at No.30, then called Carlingford House, in the autumn of 1926. Several of his literary circle visited him there and one of them noted 'how depressing and void I found the 18th-century charm of Hampstead'. George Orwell was also critical of this area in his *Keep the Aspidistra Flying*, written in the mid-1930s when he was working in a bookshop in South End Green: he immortalised this street as the 'dingy, depressing' Willowbed Road.

RUDALL CRESCENT's name was officially approved in 1877 but, as with several other developments by the British Land Company, its derivation is unknown. The most famous artist to use **Penn Studio** behind No.13 was Mark Gertler (see plaque), who came here in 1915 and stayed for 17 years. From an East End Jewish family, 'by his talents, vivacity and exotic beauty' says the DNB, 'he gained early entry into artistic and intellectual circles'. In this studio he entertained Lytton Strachey, gave tea to Aldous Huxley, found lodgings for D H Lawrence (see above), and painted the portrait of Sir Arthur Bliss (p 49). He later used a studio in Well Road, where he has recently been plaqued, and after his marriage in 1930 he lived in **KEMPLAY ROAD** at No.22. This is another inexplicable street name on the Carlile House estate, though traditionally all the roads were named after members of the British Land Company. When the estate was sold up, supporters of Rosslyn Hill Chapel bought up the sites of **Nos.5–7** and **13–21** to stop the chapel being 'hemmed in by houses of an inferior class'. After many years' use as tennis courts, the derelict land was bought by the Council in 1953 and these houses were built. The YWCA opened its hostel at **Nos.6–8** in 1901. Norman del Mar, congenial conductor of many a Promenade Concert, lived at **No.1a** in the 1950s.

CARLINGFORD ROAD could well be named after Lord Carlingford, who succeeded Peel as Chief Secretary for Ireland and was raised to the peerage in 1874, the year before the road was built. In 1912 another young East End artist, Isaac Rosenberg, who studied at the Slade with Gertler and Stanley Spencer, was living miserably at **No.32**. His studio-lodging was a bare room, with packing-case furniture and broken windows, and by 1914 he earned so little from his art and his poetry that he joined the army. He was killed four years later on the Somme, but his war poems are his lasting glory.

DENNING ROAD was developed from 1878, mainly by local builders Allison and Foskett. From the 1890s, **No.4** was Miss Slipper's girls' school, but the schoolgirl then at **No.25** was patronising the North London Collegiate. This was the future family planner, Marie Stopes, living here uneasily with her parents. In particular, she was embarrassed by her archaeological father bringing so many boxes of fossils into the house that the neighbours thought he was a grocer. Ms Stopes has a plaque in Well Walk. A maisonette at **No.34a** was the home in the 1930s of the Presbyterian family of Sandy Wilson, who wrote that certain thing called *The Boy Friend*. They came to Hampstead, he said, because 'it had been since the 1890s a sort of colony for expatriate Scots, the wealthier of whom built themselves pseudo-baronial mansions'. Note the sunflowers on this and adjoining houses, and the ripe pomegranates on **Nos.29–33**, with pretty canopies and the date 1880. **No.38**, long known as Denning Hall, is labelled 'Asked of God, 1883'. It was built as a Mission Hall for St Stephen's, Rosslyn Hill, but became the HQ of the local Church Lads Brigade in World War I and a dining hall for AckAck batteries on the Heath in WW II. Since then it has housed, inter alia, a Boys' Club ('tomfoolery and lackadaisical attitudes will not be tolerated'), a gym, a nursery school and a photographer's studio.

PILGRIM'S LANE takes its name from Charles Pilgrim, who owned land around here and lived in Vane House on Rosslyn Hill. The road was originally a cul-de-sac from Rosslyn Hill as far as the double bend, but around 1880 it was joined to the newer northern stretch, then known as Worsley Road. In 1968 the inhabitants of Worsley Road successfully petitioned to be included in Pilgrim's Lane and the whole street was renumbered. Two Worsleys were ministers of St John's, Downshire Hill, the parsonage of which is now **No.64**. Across the road, next to a Moroccan oasis, **No.41** was Mark Gertler's lodgings during his Rudall Crescent

period. **Nos.40–44** are on the site of St Stephen's National School, which by 1907 had become the Branch Library until that moved to Keats Grove in 1931. At the south end of the Lane, a plaque on **No.8** salutes that curious character W J Cory, Eton master ('a brilliant tutor' says the DNB), who left the school mysteriously, assumed a new surname, married a rector's daughter less than half his age, and ended his days in Hampstead teaching classics to young ladies. Best remembered now as the author of the *Eton Boating Song,* he came to Pilgrim's Lane from Cannon Place in 1891 and died here the following year.

In the 1970s, Daniel Barenboim and Jacqueline du Pré made music at **No.5a** in their sound-proof studio (see plaque). **No.7** is a late-18th-century house, which once had two service wings. Only one has survived: this is now **No.9**, Cossey Cottage. **Nos.1&3** were built by Horace Field about 1896, along with the bank at the corner. Among the first residents at No.1 were the artist (Sir) William Nicholson and his family. His son, the future abstract artist, Ben, attended a local school, Heddon Court in Shepherd's Walk (p 73). In the 1930s he returned to Hampstead to the Mall Studios in Belsize Park, where he spent 'one of the happiest periods of his life' with Barbara Hepworth and their triplets. In 1973 he was back in Pilgrim's

Lane at **No.2b**, and he died there in 1982. **No.2a**, Rosslyn Hill House, is the only house left from an early-19th-century row which stretched down to Downshire Hill. The other houses allowed shops to be built on their Rosslyn Hill frontages, and only the shops have survived. The Nevinsons, who were early occupants of Rosslyn Hill House, were a famously benevolent Hampstead family and progenitors of H W, the 'Grand Duke of journalism', and his artist son, C R W Nevinson, the apostle of Futurism. Resident in Pilgrim's Lane for over 30 years have been Michael Foot and his wife, Jill Craigie, distinguished in politics and cinematics respectively.

The Downshire Hill triangle, embracing Keats Grove and the upper part of South End Road, is one of the great pleasures of Hampstead. A satisfying number of the stuccoed brick Regency villas have survived, mostly in well-kept terraces with rich gardens in front (Fig 15). Nearly all of them have stayed family houses, avoiding relegation into flats and lodgings, and most are Listed buildings, as a 'group of considerable merit'. In its early days, the area was known as the Lower Heath Quarter, or sometimes as the Brickfield. Apart from this industry, there is some evidence of the existence of cottages and farm buildings here on the edge of the

Heath before the developers arrived.

DOWNSHIRE HILL was a dignified development of the early 19th century. Its exact date of birth is not recorded, but it must have been just before 1814, when the southern part appears on Park's map of Hampstead. The street name, first seen in the 1819 Rate Books, perhaps relates to the first Marquis of Downshire, with the apt family name of Hill, who achieved some fame as Secretary of State for the colonies and, in particular, for his harsh policy towards America.

At the south-west end, **No.1b**, dated 1891 on its front, started as a postal sorting office, became a Social Security office, served as a Muppet factory from 1974 and now, since 1997, has been the Keats Group Medical Practice. (The poet's name was also adopted for a nearby restaurant, but Byron has now supplanted him.) The original villas begin with **Nos.4–6**, all bow-fronted and balconied, and continue with **Nos.7–8**, all Gothic and crenellated. During World War I, No.6 was the home of the literary Garnett family, Edward, Constance and David. The poet Edwin Muir lived at No.7 in the early 1930s and described its plumbing and other problems in his autobiography; but he forgave the house its troubles as he was 'in love with its sweet, battered, Mozartian grace'. In the late 1930s, this was the home of tennis champion Bunny Austin. At the turn of the century Gordon Craig, the revolutionary stage designer, shared rooms in No.8 with composer Martin Shaw. Though already married, Craig eloped with Elena Meo, the daughter of an artist who lived across the road at No.30. The latter was reconciled to his daughter only by the intervention of Craig's mother, the great actress Ellen Terry, who regarded Elena as her 'favourite daughter-in-law'. **No.9**, the self-styled Manor House, is reputedly the oldest house in the street. The poet Sylvia Lynd (née Dryhurst) was born at **No.11** in 1887: one of her poems described the house's wonderful wisteria. After her marriage to Robert Lynd, they moved to **No.14** until 1918 and later to Keats Grove.

No.14a Downshire Hill introduces a sudden classical note into this Georgian row – perhaps because it was built as a temple of learning for nearby St John's. Founded by the minister, the Rev John Wilcox, in the early 1830s, the school grew rapidly and by 1846

15 Downshire Hill 1842, engraving by Harwood.

accommodated 96 boys and 60 girls. By 1885 it had become St Stephen's National School, which was later extended into Pilgrim's Lane (p 54). The 'temple' took on a new lease of life during World War I as the studios of the Carline family. Based at No.47, they were not only artists themselves, but attracted a large circle of modern painters, alternatively known as the Hampstead Set or the Downshire Hill Group. Hilda Carline became Stanley Spencer's first wife and he, together with Henry Lamb, Mark Gertler, C R W Nevinson, Robert Bevan and many others, would meet here and at No.47 to paint and talk and, at least once, throw a fancy dress party for 200 people. The place seemed to appeal to artists, as Richard Carline said, 'especially at mealtimes'. Pevsner called the original 1835 house 'demonstratively Grecian', but it was radically rebuilt in 1989 with a luxury appendage called **Heath Villa**.

Nos.16–17 are labelled **Portland Place** and dated 1823, while **Nos.18–19** have an illegible name plaque which once said Weymouth Place. **No.20** is notable for its cast-iron balconies, a splendid feature of this street, and two fire insurance plaques. Before World War II, **No.21** was the home of art expert Sir Roland Penrose, and after the war of John Bainbridge, the versatile Australian artist. Between **Nos.23** and 24 is the entrance to what was the Hampstead Heath Riding School and, before that, livery stables. In 1873 Walter Hill, son of the local publican, is shown as a cab proprietor here and in 1885 his brother William is licensed to hire dog carts and tricycles. The horses moved out in 1962.

In their early days, **Nos.25–26** were known as Langham Place, and the former was briefly the home of John Constable and his family. The artist was already in the habit of coming to Hampstead for the summer at least, and had rented four different local houses, notably one in Lower Terrace, before choosing Downshire Hill in 1826. Writing to his friend C R Leslie in December that year, he says: 'We are in No.1 Langham Place, Downshire Hill, a spot in a valley just before you enter the town. Our house is to the left of the new chapple (sic).' No.25 was also the home in the 1980s of scientist Sir Peter Medawar, 'last of the great polymaths', whose work on skin grafts won him a Nobel Prize in 1960.

No.31 Downshire Hill figures in the Minutes of the Vestry (the forerunner of the parish council) of 1873 because it overlooked Tibbles' Yard and the householder complained about the pigs and refuse. 'The smell is very bad,' he wrote, 'and the lodgers won't stop.' But there were no complaints from **The Freemasons' Arms**, which is first mentioned in the Rate Books of 1819. Frequently rebuilt and extended to cater for modern tastes and thirsts, the latest main revision was in 1936 and involved battles with the River Fleet, which flows underneath. The pub was once famous for its Pell Mell court. It was originally a Flemish game imported by Charles II after his exile and introduced in Pall Mall, which soon took the name of the game. Played in the open, the game involved heavy balls held by rings at the end of poles and thrown through round hoops on a swivel. The pub basement has, however, kept its old skittle alley, which is the last of its kind in London.

Across the road are further cottages of the early- and mid-19th-century variety. Professor J D Bernal, physicist and philosopher of science, lived at **No.35** in the late 1930s: among his many achievements was the design of the Mulberry Harbours for the last war's D-Day. **No.36** was Sir Roland Penrose's post-war home, and **No.37** Flora Robson's pre-war prestigious address. After her success as Elizabeth I in *Fire over England* in 1936, she was put under contract by Alexander Korda, which allowed her to take 'a smart house in Downshire Hill, buy a car and engage a chauffeur'. Tony Greenwood, Baron Greenwood of Rossendale, who lived at **No.38**, was *inter alia* Labour's Minister of Housing in the late 1960s. During his Cabinet days, he had an office built in the garden with his own scrambler phone link to No.10 Downing Street. **Nos.39 and 40** and the terraced **Nos.41–43** were all built in 1825 and by 1849 were owned by the Duke of Devonshire. Nos.39 and 41 were at various times the home of Italian artist Gaetano Meo and his large family, one of whom fell in love with the occupant of No.8. Meo began as the much-loved model of Dante Gabriel Rossetti and other Pre-Raphaelites, notably Henry Holiday, who made him his assistant at his Redington Gardens studio (p 22). Meo's poor English was occasionally a problem: he captioned a Holiday cartoon of *Moses in the Bullrushes* as *Moses in the Bull and Bush.* Meo died at No.41 in 1925 but his daughter, Taormina, owned the house until 1957. The author and advocate of women's rights Amber Blanco White, who lived at **No.44**, was a close friend of H G Wells (see Church Row, p 78) and bore him a daughter: he modelled his *Ann Veronica* on her New Woman.

At the fork with Keats Grove, the centrepiece of this area is the splendidly situated **St John's Church, Downshire Hill**. Most local histories say that the building dates from 1818, but the present church was definitely not opened to public worship until 1823. The church guide suggests that its builder, William Woods from Kennington, was also its designer. Woods, who developed much of the Downshire Hill area, using quantities of local bricks from old farm buildings and brickfields, built a very similar chapel in North Brixton. The church, with its elegant portico and cupola, galleries and box pews, is a delight both outside and in (and is now Listed grade I). Like the old Well Walk chapel, it was probably intended as a chapel-of-ease to Hampstead Parish Church, also dedicated to St John, but it became a proprietary chapel (that is, privately owned), and is now the last of its kind in London.

Among Downshire Hill's many artistic associations, **No.47** was the home of the Carline family (see No.14a), who lived here from 1914 to 1936. Richard Carline (1896–1980) was prime mover of the Hampstead Artists' Council, founded in 1944, and became UNESCO's first art consultant in 1945: he appears as a reviving corpse in Stanley Spencer's *A Cookham Resurrection,* painted in the Vale of Health. Just before World War II, No.47 became the headquarters of the Artists' Refugee Committee under Stephen Bone, much helped by Diana Uhlman and her husband Fred, artist and author. One refugee, who was invited to lodge here for 2 weeks and stayed for 5 years, was the German Dadaist John Heartfield, credited with the invention of photo-montage.

The ground drops away behind **No.49**, which has its entry at first-floor level, and this may have prompted the baseless belief that the house was a hunting lodge that pre-dates the street. The poet, Anna Wickham, one of D H Lawrence's circle, lived here during World War I and wrote a poem about the house. In the 1960s this was the home of architect and town-planner, Sir Frederick Gibberd, responsible for such epics as London Airport and Harlow New Town. The glass box at **No.49a** caused some local apoplexy when it was built by Sir Michael Hopkins in 1978, but it received a Civic Trust Award the following year and was praised for its 'refreshing clarity and panache'.

Next door is one of the first blocks of flats in the area, **Hampstead Hill Mansions**, showing its building date, 1896. Its famous residents have included (Dame) Peggy Ashcroft in 1946. On the site of this block was Spring Cottage, where Rossetti spent a short time in lodgings with Lizzie Siddal, soon after their marriage in 1860. Lizzie already liked Hampstead, as she had convalesced here after posing for long hours in the bathtub for Millais's *Ophelia.* Rossetti, on the other hand, had said that Hampstead was 'pretty well beyond civilisation'. The mid-19th-century **No.50** was in recent years the home of Jim Henson, master muppeteer, whose factory was across the road. The final building at the top of the street was Hampstead Magistrates' Court, built in 1934 and closed in 1998. Among notable literary ladies in Downshire Hill have been Olive Schreiner, Mabel Quiller-Couch and Elizabeth Jenkins.

KEATS GROVE has also kept many of its Regency villas and cottages intact. Much of the north side dates from about 1820, as Keats himself confirmed in a letter that year from Wentworth Place: 'The half-built houses opposite . . . seem dying from old age before they are bought up.' The first name for the street was Albion Grove, seen on the 1829 map, but soon after it became John Street, probably in reverence to St John's Church. It was not until 1910 that the road was named after its most famous resident. Orwell called it Coleridge Grove in *Keep the Aspidistra Flying*.

No.1, with an attractive Gothic porch, was the home of Marjorie Rackstraw (1888–1981), founder of Hampstead Old People's Housing Trust: a block of flats in Primrose Hill Road is named after her. In the 1930s **Nos.4a and 5** were peppered with poets and critics – Louis MacNeice and Geoffrey Grigson at the former and Robert and Sylvia Lynd at the latter, with Edwin Muir just up the road. Grigson founded and edited his magazine *New Verse* here, and called one of his prose poems *Uccello on the Heath*. Among the Lynds' guests in 1931 were James Joyce and Nora Barnacle, who were married from here at Hampstead Town Hall.

No doubt all these poets were inspired by the proximity of **Keats House**. Originally known as Wentworth Place, it was built in 1815–16, one of the first houses in the street. It was a joint venture by the antiquary and critic Charles Wentworth Dilke and his friend Charles Armitage Brown, and the design ingeniously disguised the fact that it was a semi-detached or duplex villa, with two front doors. The Dilke family used the central one, and Brown had his entrance round the side. Keats moved in with Brown in 1818 after his brother, Tom, had died at their noisy lodgings in Well Walk. About this time he met Fanny Brawne and in the spring of 1819, on Dilke's departure, her family took over his part of Wentworth Place. In May that year, sitting here under a plum tree, Keats wrote his ode to the nightingale that had built its nest in the garden. At the age of 23, this was his summer of supreme poetic achievement: the rest of his story is tragedy. Consumed with tuberculosis, he left Hampstead in 1820 and died in Rome the following year. The Brawne family stayed in Wentworth Place until 1829.

Ten years later, the house was bought by Eliza Chester, a retired actress, who had also held the curious post of Reader to George IV. She converted the property into a single residence and added the new wing. The name was then changed to Lawn Cottage, and later to Lawn Bank. In 1896 the brown plaque to Keats was erected by the Royal Society of Arts, and in 1920–21 the house was rescued from demolition by public subscriptions, largely from America. (Somebody worked out that John Keats was an anagram of Thanks, Joe!) Its future was then vested in the local Council, and from 1925 it was opened to the public. The house is now managed by the Corporation of London. The tall trees along the road fence were probably planted when the house was built, and the mulberry tree is said to date from Stuart times. A plaque records the position of the historic plum tree, which has been suitably replanted, but there are no longer any nightingales.

Adjoining Keats House is the **Heath Branch Library**, designed by Sydney Trent and opened in 1931 together with the Keats Memorial Library. Keats Museum advertised on the ornate gateway (Fig 16), is no longer open.

Down the road, two bollards marked St PPM have wandered in from St Pancras and should be ignored. The Edwardian **Wentworth Mansions** also took their name from Charles Wentworth Dilke. Opposite, **No.11A** was the home (1973–83) of playwright Alan Ayckbourn. **No.12** is a 'spacious, white-walled early-19th-century house', says Roy Jenkins, in his biography of H H Asquith. The future Prime Minister came here in 1877, after his first marriage, and here 10 years later his only daughter was born, the future Lady Violet Bonham-Carter. The same year the family moved to the 'larger, less attractive' 27 Maresfield Gardens, where a plaque has now been erected.

Nos.19–22 are charming cottages, reputedly built by and for workers in the local brickfield. Dame Edith Sitwell lived briefly and died calmly at No.20 in 1964. To an enquirer after her health, she is said to have replied: 'I am dying, but otherwise quite well.' She renamed the cottage Bryher House after the novelist of that name who was her friend and patron. **No.24** displays a large Ancient Lights sign on its side wall to warn off any building that comes too near.

Two houses on the other side of the road were demolished in 1900 to make

16 *Gateway of Heath Branch Library, Keats Grove (drawing by Kassie Foss, 1992).*

way for **HEATH HURST ROAD**. The road was originally called Heathurst, but was changed in 1902 – perhaps because the residents objected to a slur on their name? **No.24** was the home of novelist Margaret Drabble from 1969 to 1995. Once dubbed the archetypal Hampstead Liberal, she reflected local life in many of her works, especially the No.24 bus route. The composer Phyllis Tate was also a long-term resident (1952–87) at **No.12**: her opera *The Lodger* (about

Jack the Ripper) was performed at the Camden Festival in 1965. The south side of this road has attracted some notable artists – Gerald Ososki at **No.7**, Anthony Eyton RA at **No.9** and cartoonist Nicholas Garland at **No.27**.

At the corner with **SOUTH END ROAD** is the oldest **bakery** in North London, bearing an 1897 plaque and the initials of its founder, William Rumbold. For many years it was a bakery-cum-post office. In a northerly direction

(the southern stretch belongs in another book), the terrace of **shops** was built in 1898 and called Station Parade. **Nos.71&73** are an impressive Regency pair, the former (Russell House) having alterations by Charles Voysey in 1890 – his earliest surviving work, said Pevsner. The **grove** of trees opposite was planted in the early 1890s over the lowest of the Heath ponds, which had become a public nuisance and was filled in. Between it and the next pond, the Hampstead Water Company sank a deep well in 1835 and installed a steam pumping engine, which they housed in an octagonal tower. This attractive pepperpot, seen in many old prints of the area (see Fig 17), later became a residence, but was demolished in 1907 because of settlement.

The **cottages** across the road are nearly all Regency, but some were badly bombed during the last war and much rebuilt. Nevertheless 'its varied houses are', said Pevsner, 'characteristic of the stuccoed architecture of the period in a setting of generous foliage'. **No.79** was the home of Annie Miller, the slum girl whom Holman Hunt groomed as a model and a prospective wife. But when she came here in 1867, she was Mrs

17 South End Road about 1900, showing the Old Engine House and part of the entrance to Hampstead Heath Station.

Thomas Thomson instead. The popular local watercolourist, Mary Hill (c.1870–1947), lived most of her life at **No.89**: her Hampstead postcards are famous, as is her delightful book *Hampstead in Light and Shade*. This house, Bronte Cottage, has kept its 19th-century name, as have several adjoining cottages. **No.97** has also kept its flight of ducks. In 1882, Alfred Harmsworth, later 'the Napoleon of the Press', found digs at **No.99.**

Studies of 19th-century censuses, published in *Camden History Review 7,*

showed that this street, known as Lower Heath, had a strong working-class element; this applied in fact to the whole Downshire Hill triangle, which did not begin gentrification until the 1920s. It is perhaps significant that **No.103** was a gardener's cottage from the 1890s to the 1920s, and then became the home of architect Oswald Milne, Alderman and Mayor of Hampstead in 1947–49.

Route 5
The Main Roads
Heath Street, Hampstead High Street, Rosslyn Hill, Fitzjohn's Avenue, and Church Row

Two main roads climb up to the centre of Hampstead. The Fitzjohns Avenue and lower Heath Street approach is a late-19th-century development, but Rosslyn Hill and the High Street follow a very ancient track. The two routes converge on the twisty upper part of **HEATH STREET**, which now makes

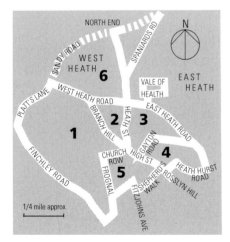

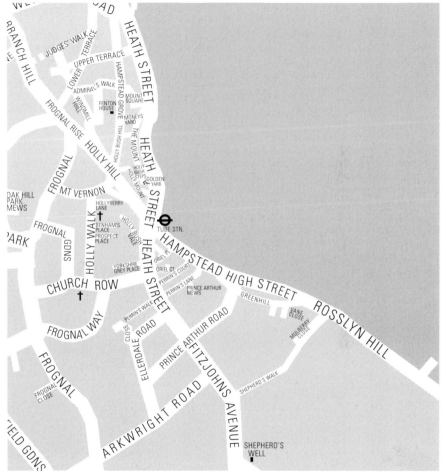

it one of the most polluted streets in London. Despite this, it is dotted with boutiques, pubs and eating houses. The street name does not appear in the Rate Books until 1831: the northern end was previously called Heath Mount and the rest was included in the High Street.

On the east side, above the Tube station (Fig 18), **Nos.58–62** are on the site of Kingswell, erected as 'a new shopping concept' in 1972. It was designed by Ted Levy, Benjamin and Partners but much revamped a dozen years later by its new owners. Ted Levy, who was not well pleased, said 'It's like trying to change a church into a disco'. The King's Well was the name of the ancient village well near here. In 1312 Robert de Kyngeswell is recorded as a free tenant of the Hampstead manor, who was nonetheless obliged to provide the lord annually with two geese and a fowl.

No.64 at the corner of Back Lane, for many years a restaurant, started its catering career in 1916 as the Tube Tea Rooms. The passage to the north led to Cornick's Yard (once belonging to a local ironmonger), where in 1903 Herbert Marnham of the Baptist Chapel benevolently provided premises for a Youth Club and Reading Rooms. From 1900 there was a gymnasium here and by 1910 it was also the first cinema in the area, variously known as The Eldorado and the Hampstead Picture Palace. **The Horse and Groom** is mentioned in records of 1723, but has been given a newer, flamboyant façade. It is now Listed, like its neighbours, **Nos.70–84**, which are all late-18th-century or early-19th-century (apart from the shopfronts). In 1900, No.76 housed two cow-keepers, and No.82 was the Ancient Smithy, offering non-chic harness, animal medicines and sanitary engineering.

The **Baptist Church**, designed by C G Searle, was opened in 1861 and used by many of the congregation

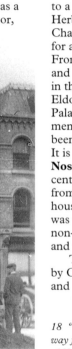

18 "Old houses bought to pull down" to make way for the Hampstead Tube station at the corner of Heath Street and Hampstead High Street.

established in the Holly Mount chapel. Much of the £6,000 or so needed for the building was supplied by a grateful merchant who had come to lodge in Heath Street in the hope that Hampstead air would cure his sick son, which it did. The site was part of Campbell's Nursery Garden, which stretched to Mansfield Place and also provided land for the mid-19th-century **Nos.86–90**, still labelled Claremont Terrace. Underneath the chapel were originally school premises specially designed for the Heath Street British Day School. Pupils were transferred to New End School in 1907. A Lecture Hall wing added to the school in 1871 on the south side has other New End connections now, as it is used by Heathside School. **Nos.92&94** are early-18th-century and among the oldest survivals in the street. **Nos.96 and 98**, which are late Georgian, were successively the addresses of E Arnot Robertson, who died here in 1961. This novelist and critic was famous for her comment that 'Hampstead is not so much a place as a state of mind'. No.98, which was called Guyon House after an old Hampstead family, was also the home from 1937 of Theodore Besterman, founder of the Guyon House Press, which produced fine books, and an authority on Voltaire (see No.6 The Mount, on the opposite side of the street). The actors Peter O'Toole and his wife, Sian Phillips, lived at No.98 for many years.

Nos.112–114 are 18th-century, but are better viewed from behind in Stamford Close. **No.118** is an early-19th-century building, which was later known as Mansfield Cottage and occupied by a gardener. From 1879 to 1887, his hermit-like lodger was Henry Sweet, author of *A History of Language*, and described by the DNB as the 'greatest British philologist and chief founder of modern phonetics': among other claims to fame, he was the original of Professor Higgins in *Pygmalion*. The **Friends' Meeting House** next door was designed in 1907 by Fred Rowntree, later responsible for the Quaker village at Jordans in Buckinghamshire. Note the 1836 Hampstead **bollard** at the entrance to Hampstead Square.

Many local parents still call **No.124**, almost at the top of the hill, Queen Mary's Maternity Home, but it is now the Geriatric Unit of the Royal Free Hospital (converted 1991). The previous building here dated back to the early-18th-century Spa period, and was known as the Upper Flask Tavern. Here met the distinguished Whig literary and social circle, the Kit Cat Club, including Pope, Addison and Steele, whose portraits by Kneller (he painted every member of the club) are in the National Portrait Gallery. This tavern also featured in Richardson's novel, *Clarissa*, published in 1748. The building became a private residence soon afterwards, and was variously called Upper Bowling Green House, or just Upper Heath. Here lived George Steevens, co-editor with Samuel Johnson of Shakespeare's works. Some gateposts and lamp-brackets and parts of the old wall of this house have survived. Lord Leverhulme (see The Hill, p 82) gave the site and Queen Mary laid the foundation stone for the model maternity home, built in 1922 with money left over from the royal comforts-for-the-troops fund of the Great War. Her Majesty took a personal interest in the home, crocheting cot covers and getting her Needlework Guilds to supply all the necessary nighties. Special layettes came from the Montreal Guild for all girls born on the Queen's birthday, who were expected to be called Mary.

Across Heath Street, behind an old wall, was the site of Heath Mount School, which originated in 1790 'for the sons of gentlemen' (see cover picture). Evelyn Waugh was a pupil here in 1911–16, as his diaries record (see also p 20), and J S Granville Grenfell, his headmaster, is supposed to be the model of the head in *Decline and Fall*. The building was demolished in 1934, but the school lives on in Hertfordshire.

On the way downhill, **Nos.115–125** make an attractive terrace, dated by the DOE as early-19th-century, but the latest DCMS List makes Nos.119 &121 early-18th-century. No.117 has half a millstone on its steps, which may well be a souvenir of the Hampstead windmills (p 32). **The Coach and Horses** has been here since 1721 but, like all pubs, has been much made over. The late-18th-century **Conduit House**, No.93, was in the greengrocery business in the 1850s, when Ford Madox Brown was painting *Work* (see p 28): the greengrocery is clearly visible in the background of the picture. **Nos.83–89** are DOE-dated as early-19th-century, but No.89 has one door inexplicably marked 'Kit Cat House 1745'. **Nos.69–81** also appear in the DOE lists, all 19th-century except No.75, which is mid-18th: most of the shop fronts have been modernised. The bar at Nos.79/81 is on the site of a famous pub 'The Nag's Head', dating back to 1698. With its decorated upper storeys the building has been Listed 'for curiosity value'. As with many properties in this shopping area, one has to look at the upper storeys to see why a building has been Listed.

19   The area between Church Row and Hampstead High Street before the Town Improvements of 1887 (plan drawn by Shirley Harris).

Between Nos.73 & 75, an alley leading up to Holly Mount (p 27) remains obstinately anonymous. After all these modest period premises, the building at

Nos.57–61 comes as a shock. It was designed by Peter Clapp for Drazin's television shop in 1970 and has been praised by the pundits for having

'guts and good manners'.

The Gothic **No.49,** with the popular clock tower, was built for a fire station by the Metropolitan Board of Works (forerunner of the LCC) in 1873, as various plaques and initials confirm. The tower was also a water tower, and this was one of the first buildings for London's new horse-drawn fire brigade to have one. Originally taller than it is now, the tower was a useful observation post in World War I, though a warning rocket was fired which unfortunately did some damage to the nearby Parochial School. The station was closed in 1915 when the new one was opened in Lancaster Grove.

Cross at the traffic lights to the **lower part of Heath Street**, which was almost entirely rebuilt, along with parts of the High Street, in 1887–89, mainly to connect the new Fitzjohn's Avenue with upper Heath Street and the High Street. Previously the way through from the south had consisted of narrow, winding and sloping courts and alleys (Fig 19), and the area had degenerated into slums. The Hampstead Town Improvements were authorised by the Metropolitan Street Improvements Act passed in 1883, and the new roads were opened to the public in February 1888, at an overall cost of £137,813. The costs were shared by the Hampstead Vestry and the Board of Works, which explains

the ownership of houses in this street by Camden Council.

Among the new buildings, the grand **Nos.23–27** on your right, designed by Keith Young, were built for Express Dairies in 1889. **Nos.15–21** also have an elaborate terracotta façade, with the date 1888 and initials GP – presumably for land-owner Major George Paget. **No.13a** provided a studio for (Sir) David Low, the New Zealand-born cartoonist, in the 1930s: then with the *Evening Standard*, he achieved fame by holding *all* political parties up to ridicule with such timeless characters as Colonel Blimp and the TUC carthorse.

Across the road, **No.24** was built by Spalding and Cross for the Hampstead Liberal Club in 1889 (see foundation stone). **The Three Horseshoes** was the name of an unlucky pub at No.62 High Street, which was displaced during the Town Improvements and rebuilt here in 1890. The rear and first floor of the pub houses the bijou **Pentameters Theatre.** Next door but one, **No.30** was built by the Wells & Campden Charity in 1889 and bears (high up) their initials, date and crest.

A number of offshoots from lower Heath Street are worth exploring. At the north-west end, **HOLLY BUSH VALE** follows the line of a pre-Improvements alley, which was linked up with a court of this name off Holly Hill about 1887.

The alley was part of Bradley's Buildings, but was entirely rebuilt. The Wells and Campden Charity erected a tenement block to accommodate some of the displaced persons on the site of **New Campden Court,** which now belongs to Camden. (Those confused by Campden and Camden should reread the *Historical Overview.*) Nearby are UCS Junior School's smart acorn-toting gates.

The **Everyman** cinema building began life in 1888 as a Drill Hall for the Hampstead Rifle Volunteers. In 1919 the windows were blocked up (but some are still visible) for Norman MacDermott's Everyman Theatre, which became one of London's leading Little Theatres. Among other premières, Noel Coward starred here in the first production (1924) of his controversial play, *The Vortex.* In 1933 the cinema was founded by James Fairfax-Jones and was run by him and his family for over 50 years. After long closure and refurbishment, 'the oldest repertory cinema in the world' was re-opened, and re-closed, in 1999.

Through the archway next door is the **Hampstead Parochial School,** the main buildings dating from 1856–62 (Fig 20), although the institution derives from the 1780s (see its history written by E V Knox). The Moreland Hall was designed in 1893 by Norman Shaw, but

66

much extended in 1938 by Ashley and Newman: it was then named after Richard Moreland, a great benefactor of the Parish Church. The Hampstead Theatre Club, now thriving at Swiss Cottage, began in this hall in 1959. They had success with Pinter premières but problems with, in the director's own words, 'the atmosphere of stale cabbage, carbolic soap and Scouts overhead'.

YORKSHIRE GREY PLACE was named in 1974 (with the help of Camden History Society) after an old inn demolished here in the 1880s. At the far end, the (invisible) **Church Row Studios** were occupied until 1988 by novelist Nicholas Mosley (son of Sir Oswald). Past Church Row (for which see p 75), the uncomfortably cobbled **PERRIN'S WALK** commemorates the Perrin family, who owned property in this area in the early 18th century, including a pub called The Goose. Until 1936, this was called Church Walk, originally consisting of coach houses for Church Row residents: the house numbers still correspond. Thus **No.24** belonged to 24 Church Row and when the artist, Norman Evill, lived at the latter between the wars, he put his initials on the Perrin's Walk frontage

20 Hampstead Parochial Schools, architect's drawing by W G and E Habershon, c.1855.

and a Strawberry Hill Gothic façade on the rear. The comedian Peter Cook moved here from Church Row in the early 1970s and stayed until his death in 1995. Hampstead was, he said, his 'magic mountain'. The picturesque **No.20** was used by Henry Holiday (see p 22) as his glassworks: the kiln chimney is still there. The versatile writer Eleanor Farjeon lived here from 1920 until her death in 1965. She is happily remembered for her children's books and the lyric of *Morning has broken*. **No.16** was converted from the coachhouse/garage of No.16 Church Row after World War I and used for a time by disabled members of the Russian Orthodox Church.

Cross Heath Street here to **PERRIN'S LANE,** also named in 1936 after many years as Church Lane. This was the main route to the church from the High Street, where No.28 was the parsonage until the 1870s. The south side of this lane has been redeveloped, but **No.8** is basically mid-18th-century and **No.12** mid-19th-century: their shopfronts have been converted to domesticity. No.12 was the home in the 1980s of Ronald Neame, the 'outstanding British cinematographer' (Halliwell). **Nos.14–26** form an attractive early-19th-century terrace. A gun-bollard dated 1828 has miraculously survived all the local

upheavals. To the south, **PRINCE ARTHUR MEWS** is first seen in the Rate Books of 1885, but the original buildings are now hardly visible. **Prince Arthur Court**, which is an exception, was intended as Model Buildings for Workers. The name of the mews recalls the opening of Monro House (see p 74) by Prince Arthur in 1869.

Return now to Heath Street and walk up the east side, quickly encountering the next sideshoot, **PERRIN'S COURT**, which was much altered at the Heath Street end during the Town Improvements. The **Village Mount** flats were built then and called Greenhill Flats: they were rebuilt and renamed after a fire in 1975. Several old houses have survived at the High Street end, including **Nos.2–6**, which are early-18th-century. Nos.2 and 4 have shopfronts, but these have been domesticated. No.2 is Listed II★ because it has kept its late-17th-century staircase. No.6 has a small original doorway and a large imported Georgian one. **Nos.1 and 3** were for many years the homes of two famous Hampstead characters. In No.1 was Bert Matthews, for 40 years rat-catcher (with dogs and ferrets) to Hampstead Borough Council and, with his wife Rebecca, Pearly King and Queen of Hampstead, while in No.3 lived the last local chimney sweep, Henry Kippin, born here in 1882 to a family of sweeps and carpet beaters. His handcart is preserved in the garden of Burgh House. **No.7** is on the site of a Temperance Hall, which became a Presbyterian Chapel and a Drill Hall and, after some rebuilding, the offices of the *Ham&High* (until 1988). A covered entrance to the north side leads to the **Hampstead Antique Emporium**, premises previously used by the White Bear Garage and, before that, by Roff and Son, the builders.

The next alley northwards, which was another builders' yard, was called **ORIEL COURT** after the nearby Oriel House. This building, with a fine orielled bay, was used for mass by the local Roman Catholic congregation before they built St Mary's, Holly Place. The house was swept away by the Improvements, along with the adjoining slum, Crockett's Court, over which was built **ORIEL PLACE**. Most of the slum dwellers were rehoused in Wells Buildings, erected in 1876 by the Wells Charity Trust (see date and initials). These were renamed **Wells Court** when 'buildings' became a dirty word. The new buildings were very much admired. In 1889 there occurred a minor outbreak of scarlet fever in Hampstead and a report made to the Vestry at that time stated that, although the buildings contained 86 children, the fever was confined to 8 cases and did not spread.

This success was attributed to the 'excellent sanitary arrangements of these buildings, together with the attention paid to ventilation and the free circulation of air occasioned by the staircases and passages being open to the air'. The tenants were not so happy about these windswept passages and 'grim-looking sub-standard' blocks in the 1960s, when Camden Council took them over and modernised them. Oriel Place has acquired two fine **lamp standards** but lost its valuable Citizens' Advice Bureau, when the Council withdrew its funding in 1991. The CAB hall (now a bagel bar) was originally part of the Liberal Club in Heath Street, but for many years was a timber merchant's.

Leading back to Heath Street, the narrow **BAKER'S PASSAGE** commemorates an old Baker's Row near here. According to Mary Hill, this latter was so called because 'Mr Baker the Curate once rode his horse down it', though the claims of Mr Burck the baker, at 59 High Street in the 1850s, seem more relevant.

From the top of Baker's Passage, walk along to **HAMPSTEAD HIGH STREET**, which in the 15th century was called Kingswell Street (see p 62), and in later years Hampstead Street and Hampstead Hill. These three names have included at times not only the present High Street but also some or all

of the upper part of Heath Street. Other names for parts of it were The Road and The Town because, from the 18th century until comparatively recently, Hampstead was not a 'village' but a 'town'. Until the Town Improvements of 1888, the High Street narrowed just above Perrin's Court to become the same width as Holly Hill. The first Improvement idea was to widen the street by demolishing the eastern side, but when the plans were submitted to the Metropolitan Board of Works a deputation of householders protested that this would make them homeless. As the western side concealed decaying property which the Vestry wished to clear away, it was then decided to remove all the buildings on that side above No.72: these had their frontages at just about the middle of the present roadway. Many unsavoury courts and alleys disappeared at the same time.

A cul-de-sac called Minerva Place survived this redevelopment, but later gave way to the Hampstead **Tube Station** (architect, Leslie Green) in 1907. In that year, the line from Charing Cross to Golders Green was opened by Lloyd George. The Hampstead platforms are the deepest in London (192 feet below ground) and became popular air-raid shelters in two world wars. Down the hill from the station **Nos.45&46**, which are 18th-century at

the back and terribly 20th-century at the front, were respectively famous for their drapery (see Mrs Siddons, p 33) and grocery businesses for over a century. McDonalds arrived at No.46 in 1993, despite strong local opposition and after a 13-year campaign for a prime site in Hampstead. They were one of several fast-food outlets, sometimes with garish façades, which invaded the High Street at that time and roused concern about the homogenisation and vulgarisation of the shopping streets. This trend to tourist-orientated enterprise, along with soaring property rents, robbed central Hampstead of most of its useful shops.

Further downhill, both Flask Walk (p 41) and **BIRD IN HAND YARD** had covered entrances (Fig 21), and the latter was particularly dangerous for drivers of the London Omnibus Company. In Victorian times, four-horse omnibuses ran regularly from here to the City and Charing Cross, roughly following the present Tube routes of the City and Charing Cross lines. Up to about 100 horses were stabled in this yard (now much curtailed) from the 1830s, and at least one drunken bus driver was nearly decapitated for failing to duck at the entrance. The alley was named after a pub at **No.39**, which was

21 Covered entry from High Street to Flask Walk, June 1903.

rebuilt in 1879 and again in the mid-1980s as a French-style café-bar, Le Dôme. This became wildly fashionable with the younger set, especially on Thursday nights, when even the pavements were packed: it was closed in 1995 as being 'past its prime'. The building's date and the bird-in-hand carving remain visible, as do the outlines of the old oil jars on **No.40**. This shop was an oil and colourman's in the 1850s and continued as an ironmonger's (Fowler's) until 1979. Fortunately, its two historic oil-jar shop-signs were then rescued for the Hampstead Museum.

On the opposite side at **No.61** (above the shop), in the mid-1930s lived and worked the artist Charles Ginner. A founder-member of Sickert's Camden Town Group, he painted several views down Flask Walk, including a joyous Coronation Day scene in 1937, which is at the Tate. Gaze's, the last of the local drapers, traded for many years at **Nos.65&66**. The bookshop (Waterstone's) at **Nos.68–69** is on a much disputed site, but the opposition to Woolworths' arrival here in the 1930s was nothing to the anti-burger battle of 50 years later. Downhill from here are older houses such as **Nos.70–72** which are basically early-18th-century. The covered entrance to Perrin's Court, much recorded by local artists, belongs to **No.73**, which was in the grocery

business for over two centuries. (Many will remember it as Forster's.) This and **Nos.74–76** are all of 18th-century origin.

The King William IV became the name of the old King's Head pub after William drove up Haverstock Hill through Hampstead in 1835 on his way to a strawberry feast at Ken Wood: his queen achieved an Adelaide Tavern and Road at the extreme foot of the hill. The mobile-looking **crêperie** beside the pub has, in fact, been stationary there for two decades. But the old red **telephone kiosk**, designed by Giles Gilbert Scott, arrived (from Camden Town) only in 1993. At **No.78** the **Hampstead Community Centre** site was first used for the pub's stables (the pub was first mentioned in 1721), and later for coachbuilders and motor engineers. This early-Victorian building was derelict in the 1970s, when the local Council bought it for a branch library (to be transferred from Keats Grove). Since 1976 they have leased it to Hampstead Community Action for a market and meeting place, the former helping to pay for the latter. The Centre now caters for locals, especially the disadvantaged, more or less from cradle to grave, including a lively After School Club and a famous Christmas Day party for pensioners. The new **post office** also arrived in the 1970s, designed by J E Jolly, taking over a site much used by

motor showrooms and, from 1883 to 1938, the offices of the *Ham&High*. The post office was due to be opened in spring 1974 by the Tory Minister of Communications, but on that very day Edward Heath lost the general election. The design was thought by Pevsner to be 'insensitive', but that of the Chinese restaurant at **No.83** (by Rick Mather) was hailed as 'elegantly modernist'. At the corner with Prince Arthur Road, **Nos.85–89** include Stanfield House, built about 1730, which commemorates the artist Clarkson Stanfield. He lived here from 1847 to 1876 (see plaque). Apart from his seascapes, which earned him the title of the English Van de Velde, he designed stage scenery, notably for amateur productions by his friend Charles Dickens: a sample is preserved at Dickens' House Museum. Many of his large family were baptised at St Mary's, Holly Place, for which he painted a portrait of Abbé Morel. Stanfield was driven away by the development of Prince Arthur Road and died in Belsize Park Gardens. The house, with a hall (by Horace Field in 1891) and other additions, was later used *inter alia* for a hospital, a school, the Hampstead Subscription Library and a Christian Science church. It is now divided into five dwellings.

PRINCE ARTHUR ROAD was partly so named in 1872, 3 years after the prince opened Monro House (p 74) The western stretch was inexplicably called Lingard Road until 1883. The 1930s blocks of **Greenhill** are on the site of a long-lived mansion called The Rookery, or Mount Grove, which was the home, until 1842, of the Longman publishing family. The house and the Greenhill estate, which was then owned by Sir John Key, a wholesale stationer and twice Lord Mayor of London, was sold by his son in 1871. A short-lived Wesleyan chapel then stood on the Rookery site until 1935, when the flats began to rise. Dame Edith Sitwell lived for 3 years at Flat 42, Greenhill (see plaque), moving in 1964 to Keats Grove, where she died.

Back up the north side of the High Street, and into the 20th century, **SPENCER WALK** is a new luxury development by the Spencer Group to designs by Ian Fraser/John Roberts. The site was also a battlefield in the 1930s, when the ancient Norway House here was demolished to make way for motor engineers, later the Blue Star Garage. **COACH HOUSE YARD** is a new name (1986) for an old yard with a new use – solicitors' offices. **No.29**, which was rebuilt after a fire in 1870 (see date), was for decades Stamp, the chemist. The bank next door, **No.28**, occupies the old parsonage, probably on the site of an even older parsonage,

first mentioned in 1660, according to Barratt. The present building dates from the early 19th century, with a baroque façade added later in the century, when God gave way to Mammon. **No.27** dates from the 18th century, but little of antiquity shows except the bootscraper in the doorway. A family firm of jewellers (Knowles Brown) left here in 1984 after nearly a century of activity. The Penfold-type **pillar box** near Gayton Road is over 100 years old and no longer in use, but it is preserved as an historic monument.

Downhill from **Nos.18&19**, an early-18th-century pair, is **MARTY'S YARD**, designed by Ted Levy in 1983: he called it 'a bit of an odd-ball development' and named it after the comedian, the late Marty Feldman, who had planned to live here. This alley was the entrance to the abattoir behind **No.17**, which for over 150 years was a butcher's. The Old Bank House, **No.14** High Street, dates back to the mid-17th century and was part of the Three Tuns Tavern in the 18th. This property then belonged to Hampstead's brewer, Robert Vincent, who also owned **The King of Bohemia**. The present pub was built in 1935, but the name is first mentioned in 1680. It is likely that the king concerned was the husband of Elizabeth of Bohemia, daughter of James I. Next to the pub is the ornate

entrance to the old brewery, established in 1720. It now leads to the peaceful **OLD BREWERY MEWS**, designed in 1973 by Dinerman Davison. The archway is part of **Nos.9 & 9A**, which

22 Heath and Old Hampstead Society plaque commemorating Maggie the flower seller (1901–1974).

have recently been Listed. The **brewery** building was converted to offices (see plaque). **Nos.6–7** High Street are on the site of Miss Noble's school, where Constable sent his daughters in the 1830s. There was a bookshop in this stretch of the High Street for over 150 years, most recently the enterprising

High Hill Bookshop, which closed in 1988. It is most remembered for the sign on its door: 'Children of Progressive Parents admitted only on Leads'.

Embedded in the wall across the road is an 18th-century **milestone** inscribed '$3\frac{1}{2}$ m from St Giles's Pound, 4 m from Holborn Bars' (the animal pound was near St Giles-in-the-Fields). **Nos.1a–c** were built with **Essex Court** on the garden of the Trinity Presbyterian Church, which was pulled down in 1962 after a century of service. Maggie Richardson, who sold flowers at this corner for 60 years, is commemorated on the east wall with a flowery **plaque** (Fig 22, p 71) designed by Gillian Greenwood.

Cross Willoughby Road to walk down **ROSSLYN HILL**, which was earlier known as Red Lion Hill after an old pub on the south side. From the early 19th century the new name, at first Roslyn (*sic*) Street, commemorated the notorious Alexander Wedderburn, Earl of Rosslyn, who in 1801 moved from Branch Hill Lodge (p 35) to a mansion in the Wedderburn Road area. On the north side, **Nos.54–66** were rebuilt in 1890 with delightful florid façades. These include the initials of the dyer and the dairyman then at Nos.66 and 62 respectively, and the proclamation of Dudman's Hampstead Borough Stores over No.56, long a grocery but now a delicatessen. On the site of these shops until 1880 was the oddly-named Chicken House, a Jacobean building, reputedly once a hunting lodge. This contained a remarkable stained-glass window (reproduced in Park and elsewhere), showing portraits of James I and his favoured Duke of Buckingham, with a French inscription stating that they stayed the night here on 25 August 1619.

At No.54 is the entrance to **PILGRIM'S PLACE** , developed in the early 19th century and named after the Pilgrim family of Vane House (p 54): the three cottages were bought by **Rosslyn Hill Chapel** in 1918. This Unitarian Chapel, built by John Johnson in 1862 and enlarged in 1885, is near the site of a chapel for Protestant dissenters dating back to 1691 (see Willoughby Road, p 52). Among the fine Victorian stained-glass windows are works by William Morris, Burne-Jones and Henry Holiday, and in the chancel are two relief panels attributed to John Flaxman. The many memorials include a tablet to the painter Helen Allingham (see her works at Hampstead Museum) and Edwin Field, the law reformer. In 1898 the chapel bought and demolished two shops in Rosslyn Hill to gain a proper entry from the main road. Their temperance campaigners also worried about the proximity of the pub at **No.48**, which went up in 1869, the year after the Red Lion came down. Until recently the pub was known as the Rosslyn Arms. **ROSSLYN MEWS**, which was George Hart's builders' yard in the 1890s, acquired some boldly modern houses in 1989. The **Lloyds Bank** building of 1896 (graded II★) is the chef-d'oeuvre of the locally active architect, Horace Field, in a style variously called Edwardian Baroque and Wrenaissance. 'It is irresistible', says Alastair Service, 'in the love and inventiveness evidently poured into its design.'

At the corner of Downshire Hill, the remarkably clean **police station**, which is No.26$\frac{1}{2}$, was built in 1913 to designs by J. Dixon Butler, a disciple of Norman Shaw. Pevsner considered it 'oversize but very pretty'. **Nos.22–24** began as a mid-18th-century mansion, but were rebuilt as two houses in the mid-19th century. **No.12** was the home of leading cubist and vorticist David Bomberg, who is well represented at the Tate.

Seventy yards further on, at the bottom of the hill, and currently at a low ebb, is **St Stephen's Church**, built in 1869 to the exuberant designs of Samuel Sanders Teulon. The site was part of the manorial waste called Hampstead Green and riddled with streams, so the foundations were never easy. But here Teulon, the rogue architect of over a hundred churches, created his *magnum* *opus* – and died, exhausted, soon after. On one Sunday in 1886, the church had 1,372 attendances. In 1977 it was made redundant and still faces an uncertain future, too expensive to demolish, even more costly to restore. Several rescue operations have recently been launched to preserve this Grade I building.

Climbing now the other side of Rosslyn Hill, we see **No.11**, built in 1740 according to one owner, and in the late 18th century according to the DOE. Called Rosslyn Grove, the house may have been the Dower House of the Earl of Rosslyn, says the one, and manse of the Congregational Church in Lyndhurst Road, says the other. More certainly, this was the home until 1932 of Hancock Nunn, Hampstead's remarkable pioneer of social service: his name is little seen now except on a block of flats in Fellows Road.

Of the Victorian houses higher up the hill, **Nos.15–41** were originally Mansfield Villas and **Nos.43–53** Rosslyn Terrace. Above here the dried-up **drinking fountain** marks the site of the Red Lion inn, after which the old road was named. The pub was demolished in 1868 and replaced by a police station. This lasted until 1913, when No.26½ (see above) was custom-built for the constabulary.

At the entrance to **VANE CLOSE**, built in 1972, a **red plaque** asserts that 'Sir Harry Vane lived here' until his beheading in 1662. This apparent time-warp is due to the surprising survival of the plaque from old Vane House, which was demolished here in 1970. Sir Harry, the 'prince of paradoxes', tried to support both sides in the Civil War and was trusted by neither. He was, said Charles II, 'too dangerous a man to let live if we can honestly put him out of the way'. Sir Harry was arrested at his Hampstead home on a trumped-up charge of treason and marched to his death at the Tower of London. His house was taken in the 1740s by the famous theologian, Bishop Butler, and from 1781–95 by Admiral Matthew Barton. Accommodated mistakenly by previous local histories at Admiral's House (p 29), Barton retired to Vane House after an exciting career. This included being shipwrecked naked on the Barbary coast and carried into slavery by the Moors. It was not until 18 months later that he was ransomed by the British Government, who promptly court-martialled him for the loss of his ship. For the last 100 years or so of its life, this house became the Royal Soldiers' Daughters Home, but they now have new premises at **No.65** and a new name, the Royal School. The institution began in 1855 as the Crimean War ended, and after 3 years in Rosslyn House the girls were marched up the hill to Vane House, led by Prince Albert. The nearby **MULBERRY CLOSE** commemorates a fine old tree in the grounds of this historic mansion which, apart from a name plaque, has been lost without trace.

Backtrack down the hill a little way to where Rosslyn Hill connects to Fitzjohns Avenue via **SHEPHERD'S WALK**, a name said to derive from local landowners called Shepherd. The **postal sorting office**, built in 1951, is on the site of St John's House, which in 1940 was, as the plaque (inside) notes, 'destroyed by enemy action'. This had previously been a boys' day school, Heddon Court, and a Cable and Wireless Training School.

The lane emerges in **FITZJOHN'S AVENUE**, where we go downhill to the next left-hand turning. A plaque in a niche marks the site of **Shepherd's Well**. This well originally produced Hampstead's purest water and was also the source of the River Tyburn, which fills the lake in Regent's Park and flows past Buckingham Palace. Turn back up Fitzjohn's Avenue, which was built in the 1870s over mainly manorial land and named after a Maryon Wilson estate in Essex. The northern, narrower stretch, which is the only part covered by this survey (see *The Streets of Belsize* for the rest), followed a well-worn route for villagers or their paid water-carriers

coming to use Shepherd's Well. Shown as Field Place on the 1832 map and as Greenhill Road on the first Ordnance Survey of 1866, it was not officially included in Fitzjohn's Avenue until 1892. The building of **No.80** (on the right) in the 1970s caused conservation rage, as
it replaced an attractive Victorian house with delightful railings. Permission had been given only for 'partial demolition', but developers removed the entire house except for one chimney stack.

Just above Shepherd's Walk is the entrance to **Fitzjohns Primary School**, founded in 1954. The handsome main building, however, dates from 1858, when it was erected as a school for the Royal Soldiers' Daughters' Home. By 1951 it had become surplus to the daughters' requirements and was sold to the LCC. Higher up, **Henderson Court** was built in 1966 as old people's flats and named after a local worthy, Sir Vivian Henderson. The concrete family group in the courtyard was made by Mary Gorrara in her Steele's Road studio: she eventually had to knock a wall down to get it out. Before world War II, **No.104** rang with strains of 'Frognal, Frognal, high on the hill', the school song of the prestigious Frognal School for Girls. In the 1920s, its ex-Roedean headmistresses were offering education

'on public school lines', including Swedish drill twice weekly. **No.114** shows its date (1878) and the initials of its first occupant, William Huson Watts, a busy builder, who suitably called this house The Hive. **No.116**, Monro House, was designed by Edward Ellis (with nautical crest) as the Royal Sailors' Daughters' Home. (The title is still on display.) This institution, which originated at 99 Frognal after the Crimean War, offered asylum for 100 girls, and education as domestic servants. The building was opened in 1869 by Prince Arthur of Connaught, who laid a memorial stone and planted a fir tree. Neither of these is visible now, but note the bird's nest over the door. The home was closed in 1957 and converted to old people's flats, named after the home's long-serving secretary, F R D'O Monro.

On the other side of the avenue, **No.79** is known as Hyelm, which is a Hostel for Young Employees of Limited Means. Arthur West House was opened in 1975 (architect: Stefan Zins) and named after the founder of the original hostel in 1926: his portrait by Frank Salisbury hangs in the hall. At the corner with Arkwright Road, the harmonious **Field Court**, commemorating Field Place, was developed for the Council in 1978 by Pollard, Thomas and Edwards. This was locally called the 'Klondike

site', after the three-fifths of an acre was sold in 1967 for £37,600 and resold five years later for five times that amount. **No.75** was built in the early 1870s by T K Green for Paul Falconer Poole, RA, painter of historic subjects. This ambitious Gothic villa is called 'a good example of its kind' by the DOE, and 'crude, elephantine' by Pevsner. There is another architectural curiosity at **No.73**, which has had an unremarkable window inserted by the mighty C F A Voysey.

Turn down **ARKWRIGHT ROAD** (derivation unknown), which was a major development in the 1870s. T K Green was the main architect of the Greenhill estate here; he designed **No.1**, now part of St Anthony's School, for himself in what Andrew Saint has called 'Ruskinian Gothic'. **Nos.2&4**, now Devonshire House School, were also by him, the latter for the then popular artist F W Topham (see plaque, if not creeper-covered). Topham was also much admired in Spain, where a square in Cordoba has recently been named 'Plaza del Pintor Topham'. The two buildings housed St Godric's Secretarial College for many years. **No.9**, dated 1874 and clearly by a different architect, was from 1909 the home of millionaire Sir Joseph Beecham, famous for his pills as well as for his son, Sir Thomas. This grand house, complete with a new wing added by Sir Joseph for a picture gallery, was bought in 1921 for £10,000 by the rich railway union, ASLEF, and has been its headquarters ever since. On the site of **Nos.11a–f** was the home in the 1930s and '40s of Sir Geoffrey Keynes, brother of Maynard and polymath extraordinary. Apart from pioneering thyroid surgery (at New End Hospital) and blood transfusions, he was a noted bibliographer and expert on William Blake. The new houses here, as well as **Nos.36a–e**, are by local architect L J Michaels. The delightfully decorated **No.13**, Welford House, was built by Green in 1878, reputedly for an Express Dairy executive. Welcome greenery fronts the adjoining new houses.

The blue plaque on **No.21** salutes Tobias Matthay, who lived here from 1902 to 1909. It must be the only official plaque to a piano teacher, but the Matthay method, taught by him at the Royal Academy of Music for over 50 years, entitled him, as one critic said, to a 'prominent position in the pantheon of pianoforte pedagogues'. **No.27** was briefly the home of actor (Sir) Ralph Richardson in 1924. On the way downhill, note the dragon on the copper dome of **No.28**, a Listed building designed by R A Briggs in 1891. At the foot of the hill, **Camden Arts Centre** was built in 1897 as Hampstead's first Central Public Library. The site was more or less in the centre of the old borough.

The building, designed in domestic Tudor style by Arnold Tayler, was twice bombed in the last war. The library transferred to Swiss Cottage in 1964.

Back up the hill, **ELLERDALE ROAD**, also on the Greenhill estate, had its name approved in 1872, though the southern leg was called Manners Road until 1881. Like Arkwright, Ellerdale sounds North Country but has no known derivation. **No.24,** built as Briarlea in 1873, with *Vivat Veritas* over the door, came to life in 1898 with the new King Alfred's 'Co-Educational and Open Air' School. King Alfred's name was adopted because he chose to educate his daughters as well as his sons. The school's aim 'to develop the natural capacity of every individual', with no competitions or marks, and no religious instruction, appealed particularly to local artistic families such as the Farjeons and the Rothensteins. The school transferred to North End Road in 1921. On the east side, **No.9** was the home of duettists Anne Ziegler and Webster Booth in the 1950s (see also p 16). **No.12** offered Board Residence in the 1930s, under the title The Yellow Door, and with the curious slogan *Food You Remember, Beds You Forget.*

Nearby **ELLERDALE CLOSE** was developed in the mid-1930s and designed by Clough Williams Ellis. The first resident at **No.1** was the journalistic

author, Beverley Nichols, whose *Green Grows the City* described Hampstead and this house and garden – and the local fogs which 'by the time they get to the top of the hill have shed much of their viciousness'.

Several 19th-century houses in Ellerdale Road have terracotta sunflowers on them, the symbol of sweetness and light. **No.6** has decorative foliage and a handsome canopy over its front door. This grand house, showing its date (1875), was designed by the great Norman Shaw for himself and he lived here until his death in 1912: he is buried in the parish churchyard. During his residence here, he designed New Scotland Yard and the Piccadilly Hotel and several local houses, including 61 Fitzjohn's Avenue. In the 1930s, No.6 became a hotel called Hampstead Towers and this name has survived, but the building is now run as a seminary by the Sisters of St Marcellina: they are also at **No.2**, a defiantly Gothic house, with delightful detail, built for himself about 1890 by the energetic T K Green. It was DOE listed 'for curiosity value'.

At the top of Ellerdale Road turn left and left again into **CHURCH ROW**. Though not a main road in the sense of a major thoroughfare – and all traffic should really be barred here – Church Row is certainly the handsomest street in Hampstead. Nearly all the houses are of early-18th-century origin, with flush-framed windows, and are Listed II★. Though many have been rebuilt or refaced they have kept up their period appearances with decorative fanlights, canopies and wrought-iron work. The Town Improvements did not improve the east end of the street, where Nos.1–4 disappeared and, in 1898, **Gardnor Mansions** arrived (the Gardnor family owned land here), one of the first blocks of flats in central Hampstead. Among the flat-dwellers in the 1920s was Margaret Llewelyn Davies (see also p 37) and, in the 1930s, Gracie Fields.

The narrow **No.5** (see Fig 23), which was weatherboarded in the late 18th century, was recently reconverted to a residence from the offices of Shepherd the builder: the asking price in 1982 was £100,000 and in 1996 £675,000. (Prices for larger houses in the street are currently nearer £4 million.) Around 1800, **No.8** was the home of two famous but now forgotten writers – Mrs Barbauld, whose husband was a minister at Rosslyn Hill Chapel, and her niece, Lucy Aikin, who loved Hampstead because 'neighbours do not think it necessary, as in the provinces, to force their acquaintance upon you'. The distinguished painter, Donald Towner, died here in 1985. (See his local views at Burgh House.) **No.9** was a Girls' Reformatory School in the 1860s and '70s and a Field Lane Industrial School for Girls (transferred here from Saffron Hill, Holborn) in the 1880s and '90s. **No.12**, which is late-18th-century, was for long the home of Geoffrey Hutchinson, QC, later Lord Ilford, who successfully fought on behalf of the Heath and Old Hampstead until his death here in 1974. Sir Norman Collins, who lived at **Mulberry House** at the west end of the street, left the BBC to champion commercial broadcasting, for which he coined the euphemism Independent Television: he also wrote the popular novel *London Belongs to Me*. Up to the end of the 19th century, a toll had to be paid at a gate across Church Row, at its junction with Frognal Gardens (p 18), since the right of way through to Frognal belonged to the Old Mansion (p 16). Across the road, **No.14** has been the vicarage of St John-at-Hampstead since the 1930s.

The present **Parish Church** was built in 1747 by John Sanderson on the site of a medieval church which had become unsuitable and unsafe for Hampstead's burgeoning population. As early as 1710, the congregation had been petitioning Parliament for repairs or replacement, as they could not 'come to Divine Service without Apparent Hazard of their lives'. The new church was dedicated to St John the Evangelist: its predecessor had been St Mary's.

After various extensions by Robert Hesketh, the church was enlarged and re-orientated in 1878, to plans by F P Cockerell. As a result, the chancel and altar are at the west end, an arrangement not much found except in Hampstead and St Peter's in Rome. The church has some fine stained glass by Clayton and Bell, and memorials to Keats and other local celebrities. The churchyard is full of famous names, and 20 graves have been Listed, including those of Constable, John 'Longitude' Harrison, George du Maurier and Norman Shaw. All the other remarkable tombstones have been surveyed, recorded and illustrated in the Camden History Society booklet *Buried in Hampstead* (available at the Church's office and elsewhere). The entrance gates were brought in 1747 (see plaque) from the Duke of Chandos's residence, Canons Park in Edgware, where Handel composed his 'Chandos Anthems'.

On the south side of Church Row, next to a lane leading to Frognal Way (p 15), **No.15** is a remarkably harmonious addition to the Georgian terraces: it was erected only in 1924 by

23 Church Row looking east, 1886, showing Oriel House in what is now Heath Street and, centre left, the site of Gardnor Mansions. From a watercolour by Harold Lawes.

Sydney Tatchell. **No.17** was the home in 1909 of H G Wells – or rather of his wife and sons, as the author had just eloped with Amber Reeves (see No.44 Downshire Hill). He returned to the family in 1910, and is shown in the local directory of that year as a JP, but his two novels published in 1910 (*The History of Mr Polly* and *The New Machiavelli*) were both about husbands fleeing unfortunate marriages. The Wells family left Church Row for Essex in 1912. The comedian Peter Cook lived here around 1970. **No.18** has a plaque to J J Park, who wrote the first history of Hampstead in 1814, and to his father, who must have helped him, as J J was only 19 at the time. **No.19** was the home, until his death in 1979, of Sir Frank Soskice, later Lord Stow Hill, who succeeded Henry Brooke as Home Secretary when Socialists took over from Tories in 1964: he was a grandson of Ford Madox Brown. New trees were presented to Church Row in 1876 by three architects living at **Nos.20, 24 and 26** respectively: Thomas Garner, G F Bodley and George Gilbert Scott Jr. Another architect in Scott's office, Temple Moore, helped to plant them, but all have now been supplanted. In 1998 a new tree was added to the central reservation (see plaque) to celebrate the Heath & Hampstead Society's centenary the previous year and to commemorate

one of its devoted chairmen, John Carswell. Two noted artists worked at No.20 – Henry Holiday in the 1890s, and Randolph Schwabe in the 1930s and 40s: he was then principal of the Slade School. **Nos.24–28** are, according to the DOE, 'early-19th-century, refaced later-19th-century Georgian style'. No.24 has a *fleur de lys* cut in the first-floor brickwork, which was the trade mark of C B King, a builder who specialised in neo-Georgian work in Hampstead (see Elm Row, p 47). His offices were at No.28. G G Scott Jr's son, (Sir) Giles, was born at No.26 in 1880. At the age of 22 he won the competition to design the Liverpool Anglican Cathedral. Later celebrities here included William Rothenstein, whose son (Sir) John went to King Alfred's, Lord Alfred Douglas and wife (1907–10) and, in the 1950s, Ludovic Kennedy and Moira Shearer. No.27 was the home of George du Maurier (1870-74) whose son, (Sir) Gerald, was born here in 1873, and of the folk song and dance expert, Cecil Sharp (1915–18).

At the Heath Street end of Church Row, No.28 deserves a book to itself. A Catholic school in the 1850s gives way to a Home for the Rescue of Young Women in the 1860s, which is replaced (or renamed) in the '70s by a Female Servants' Home. The builders move in by the '90s, when it was C B King's

office, and are soon joined by various artists including Muirhead Bone, who in 1910 lets his flat (without bathroom) to Compton Mackenzie at £4 per month. The author describes in *Octave 4* how an etching of Bone's he found in the flat gave him the title of one of his earliest successes, *Sinister Street*. Finally, from 1908 this was the office of the Women's Cooperative Guild and Margaret Llewelyn Davies, whose visitors included Leonard and Virginia Woolf. The latter often came to the 'immaculate and moral heights of Hampstead' and admired its 'uncompromising and high-minded' inhabitants, many of whom she must have found among the delights of Church Row.

Route 6
The Outskirts
North End Way, Spaniards Road and the Vale of Health

Start from the Whitestone Pond at the top of Hampstead Hill, where on a clear day there are breathtaking views to east and west. **NORTH END WAY** takes over here from Heath Street and at the fork in front of Heath House leads left down to the borough border. At the summit you are at the highest point in North London, 440 feet above sea level,

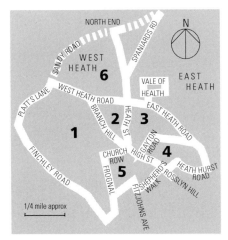

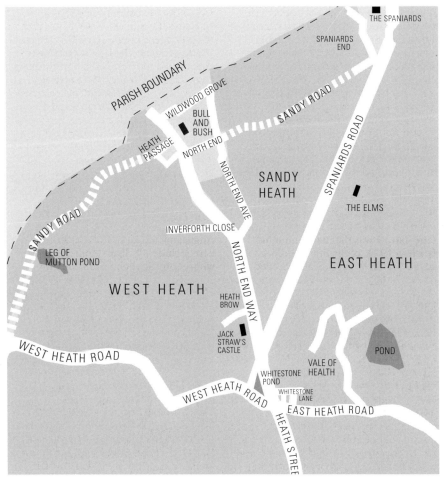

and about 20 feet higher than the cross on the dome of St Paul's. The clumps of bushes on the south side were originally planted to discourage the donkey touts of Victorian times. Here they had their stands and offered rides on some of the 'hundred Hampstead donkeys' (Fig 24). It was George du Maurier who nicknamed **Whitestone Pond** 'Ponds Asinorum'. Among the bushes beside the pond is the old white **milestone** after which the pond is named. The faded inscription reads on one side '4½ miles from Holborn Bars', and on the other 'IV miles from St Giles's Pound'. Ramps at either end of the pond show that horse-drawn vehicles used to drive right through this rainwater pond. After climbing Hampstead Hill, horses could refresh themselves here before their drivers did the same at the local inn. For many years, children used to paddle here and sail their boats, but the area is now a dangerous, polluted traffic complex. On the Heath below the road, to the east, is a disused brick **pinfold** or cattle pound (Fig 25), which dates from 1787 and is a Listed rarity.

On the West Heath side of the pond, a **flagstaff** (recently replaced in fibreglass) marks the site of the Armada beacon, one of a chain of signal fires in Elizabethan times, notably in 1588, when a Spanish invasion was threatened. 'High on bleak Hampstead's swarthy moor, they started for the north', wrote Macaulay in *The Lay of the Spanish Armada*. The first flagstaff was erected by the Lord of the Manor about 1845 and flew his flag (the cross of St George) whenever a Manorial Court was being held. The **Old Court House** is the name of the house to the north, but there is no evidence of courts being held here, or that this was, according to one story, where Judge Jeffreys 'persecuted his prisoners'. The house was built in the 1780s by the owner of the adjoining tavern, where Manorial Courts were in fact held every Whitsun and Christmas, and which in the 19th century became

24 *Donkey rides near Whitestone Pond (drawing by John Leech, 1860).*

the Manor Estate Office. The Lord of the Manor also lodged here on his rare visits to Hampstead. Earlier called Heath View and Earlsmead, the Old Court House was converted to senior citizens' flats in the 1960s.

Jack Straw's Castle, views of which in two centuries are shown in Figs 26 and 27, can claim to be the highest pub in London and hence to have been patronised by the highest in the land. Its name, however, is a misnomer. The notorious Jack Straw of the Peasants' Revolt of 1381 almost certainly never came here, and there never was a castle. But by 1713, when the tavern's name was first mentioned, there had been a revival of interest in the semi-legendary peasant rebel, and at least two plays were written about him. The pub was badly bombed in the last war and rebuilt in 1962 by Raymond Erith, with a comically castellated front. Charles Dickens and Karl Marx were frequent customers here.

The **war memorial**, dating from 1922, was extended in 1953 and moved from the middle of the road to ground donated by the owners of **Heath House** behind it. This early 18th-century mansion was bought in 1790 by Samuel Hoare, the Quaker banker, whose family

25 The pound on the Heath in the dip close to Gangmoor.

took a squirely interest in Hampstead for over a century. They were instrumental in starting schools, relieving the poor, building churches and saving the Heath. They also entertained William Wilberforce here to further his anti-slavery campaign and discussed prison reform with Elizabeth Fry. The house got its present name when taken in 1888 by the newspaper proprietor Sir

Algernon Borthwick, later Baron Glenesk. He was succeeded here by the Guinness family, one of whom became the Earl of Iveagh in 1919 and moved to Ken Wood. Heath House, which then passed to his third son, created Baron Moyne in 1932, has not surprisingly been called 'a veritable breeding place for the peerage'.

A cluster of cottages called

Littleworth grew up behind Jack Straw's Castle in the 18th century, but by 1800 the smallholders had been swept away by a wave of Whig aristocracy. The new residents included Lady Crewe, Lady Camelford and Lord William Grenville, leader in 1806-7 of the government which abolished the slave trade. The villas, which grew to prestigious size, were mostly destroyed by a parachute mine in 1941 and their grounds were added to the Heath. Some of their garden **trees** can still be seen between the pub and Inverforth House. The road leading to the car park behind the pub was called Heathbrow and led to a villa of that name, finally flattened in World War II. At the corner with North End Way, a **stone** records the success of the Hampstead Heath Protection Society in adding half an acre to the Heath in 1925.

On North End Way, towards Golders Green, **Inverforth House** swallowed up a smaller house called The Hill, which was given by Samuel Hoare to his son in 1807, when the latter married Elizabeth Fry's sister. The black plaque records that John Gurney Hoare, who was born here in 1810, took a leading part in the battle to save the Heath from development. The Hill was bought in 1906 by William Lever, later Lord Leverhulme, the son of a Bolton grocer who made his fortune from Sunlight Soap. He rebuilt the house,

added two wings (one for his art gallery), acquired two neighbouring properties, Cedar Lawn and Heath Lodge, laid out new grounds designed by Thomas Mawson, and built the pergola walk. He found it inconvenient that the Heath Lodge part of his estate, now The Hill Garden, was separated from the rest of his property by a public footpath, but all Leverhulme's powers and riches could

not buy him this right-of-way. He made many national and local benefactions, but died in 1925 still worth £57 million. Lord Inverforth, the shipping magnate, began living at The Hill the following year and in 1955 bequeathed it to Manor House Hospital. In 1996–8 it was converted to luxury apartments, the largest then priced at £4½ million.

After you pass this development,

INVERFORTH CLOSE leads to the splendid but rather secret **Hill Garden**, which is now open to the public, as is the delightful **Pergola Walk**, now Listed II★. The earthen foundations for this were spoil from the Underground's Northern Line excavations.

Continue down the pathway high above the **cutting** in North End Way, probably dating from the 1730s. This was formerly famous for its Gibbet Elms, which stood just to the north of The Hill for many years. Here in 1673 was hanged the villainous highwayman Francis Jackson, and his skeleton was left dangling in chains for another 18 years as a warning to others. The last of these elms was blown down as recently as 1907.

The hamlet of **North End** is presumed to be the Sandgate mentioned in Hampstead's charter of 986 (Sandy Heath is very near), and from Tudor times it is often referred to as Wildwood Corner. This is the name in William Camden's *Britannia* of 1695.

North End has long been famous for its two pubs, both of which are mentioned in the Holborn Register of 1730. **The Bull and Bush**, popularised by Florrie Forde's song, developed from a farmhouse reputedly built about 1645.

26 (Left) Jack Straw's Castle, 1834 (drawing by T H Shepherd).
27 (Right) Jack Straw's Castle, c.1906.

The young William Hogarth lived here and laid out the gardens, which became a popular attraction of the tavern (see Fig 28). Gainsborough, who drank here with Reynolds and Garrick, called it 'a delightful little snuggery'. Of the many theories about the name, the most likely derives the 'bull' from the farm and the 'bush' from the ivy bush that was a tavern sign. The present building dates largely from 1924 but the two front bay windows are certainly older. **The Hare and Hounds**, which was twice bombed in 1940 and existed for a time in five linked caravans, was rebuilt in 1968. Its pub sign has been highly commended (except by those who deplore blood sports).

Beyond the borough boundary and the entrance to **Golders Hill Park**, which was added to Hampstead Heath

83

in 1899, is **Ivy House**, where ballerina Anna Pavlova lived from 1912 to 1931 (see plaque). Golders Hill was saved by public subscription, and enough money was raised to buy an additional patch for the Heath opposite the Bull and Bush. This was the site of an old terrace called Ambridge Cottages, two of which have survived. One has kept the name of the terrace and the other is known as **Briar Cottage**. The western leg of **SANDY ROAD** starts near here and soon comes to **No.9**, which was the North End School built by John Gurney Hoare in 1849 and managed by his youngest daughter, Margaret. The bell is still under the eaves, and a homily about training a child 'in the way he should go' is still visible on the roof line. **No.8** was the home of character actor Nigel Stock, who died here in 1986: he was a memorable Dr Watson in a TV Sherlock Holmes series.

Further on, the road turns into a track and passes the **Leg o'Mutton Pond**, the name descriptive of its shape. The roadway was made by some parish paupers in 1825 as part of a job creation scheme devised by Mr Hankins, a Poor Relief Supervisor. The project was soon known as Hankins' Folly. To the east of the pond a **mesolithic site** has recently

been excavated, and considerable information unearthed about Early Man in Hampstead (see display in the Hampstead Museum). This was evidently the camp site of some forest hunters in 7000 BC. The narrow **HEATH PASSAGE** leads back to the main road. In the 1950s, **No.4** was the studio of Russian-born Boris Anrep, who designed the new mosaic floor for

the National Gallery foyer. The continuation of Sandy Road on the east side of North End Way has been called **NORTH END** since 1942. **Nos.1&3** are an early-18th-century pair, and **Wildwood Lodge** is a mid-19th-century Gothic *cottage orné*. This last house, which was owned in 1869 by Queen Victoria's dentist, sports a Victorian frontage to two old cottages, all now

28   The Bull and Bush, c.1906. Note the entrance to the tea gardens, now a car park.

obscured by holly trees. Its wall and gateway (with overthrow) have recently been Listed and its garden has sprouted some new houses under the name **PARFITT CLOSE**.

In **NORTH END AVENUE**, a plaque on the gate to new **Pitt House** records its remarkable predecessor, bombed in world War II and demolished in 1952. Variously known as Wildwoods and North End Place, the house was used in 1767 for convalescence by the Prime Minister, William Pitt, Earl of Chatham. He was so sick in body and mind that he shut himself away in a top room and refused to see anyone: all his food was served through a hatch. George III was so worried that at one point he threatened to visit Pitt at North End himself. In 1905–1908 this was the home of newspaper proprietor Harold Harmsworth, later Lord Rothermere, and from 1914 of the Fleming family, whose famous sons, Ian and Peter, were brought up here. To the south, the grounds of Pitt House have been absorbed in the Heath, including an old **arch** which linked parts of the garden. A plaque credits the design of the arch to John Paine. The old garden wall has been Listed.

Across the avenue, attractive **Cedar Lodge** is mainly 18th-century. This was known as Myrtle Lodge or Myrtlewood until Lady Byron came to live here in 1908 and it became Byron Cottage. She was the wife of the 9th Lord Byron, known as 'red-nosed George', and only distantly related to the poet. He was one of a succession of rich husbands for this ex-chorus-girl, whom Churchill described as 'the modern Boadicea'. In 1924 she married Sir Robert Houston, a shipping magnate and, as Lady Houston, was noted as one of the wealthiest women in the country. Among other causes, she poured money into the struggling British aircraft industry, which greatly helped the development of the Spitfire engine. This is why one of her biographers called her 'the Woman who Won the War'.

Round the corner, **No.23** North End, known as North End Lodge, has been dated about 1760, but the local artist Mary Hill, who lived there a century ago, claimed that part was as old as Queen Anne.

At the crossroads, an old **boundary stone** dated 1833 appears to have slipped a bit, as the borough boundary is about 100 yards to the north. In this direction are the totally tile-hung **Wildwood** and **No.15**, an 18th-century farmhouse divided up in 1809. Across the road, **No.19** was built in 1953 by the young architect Michael Ventris, famous in archaeological circles for having decoded the Cretan hieroglyphics known as Linear B (see blue plaque).

To the north is **Wildwood Terrace**, architecturally unremarkable except for the residence at **No.2** in 1936–83 of Sir Nikolaus Pevsner (see black plaque). This indefatigable art historian, who has opened so many eyes to the joys and quirks of architecture, will be best remembered by his Domesday Survey of *The Buildings of England* in 47 volumes, a project that could not have been completed without the financial support of the Leverhulme Trust (see above). Behind here is another Victorian terrace called **WILDWOOD GROVE**, first mentioned in the 1873 Directory. In the 1950s, **No.5** was the home of actor-manager Donald Wolfit, whose parts at this period ranged from Tamburlaine at the Old Vic to Captain Hook at the Scala.

In all the wilds of North End, the most picturesque place is **Wyldes** itself, bestriding the border of Hampstead and Hendon. The two houses, now called Old Wyldes and Wyldes, were respectively the farmhouse and barn of the 340-acre estate: the farmland has been absorbed by Hampstead Heath Extension and Hampstead Garden Suburb. In medieval times, the estate was owned by the leper hospital of St James (where St James's Palace now stands), and for 370 years it belonged to Eton College. From c.1785 to 1854 the farm was let to the Collins family and took their name, though it was also variously known as Heath Farm and Wildwood Farm. From 1824–28, the young artist, John Linnell, was lodging here with his family and was often visited by his future son-in-law, Samuel Palmer, and by the aged William Blake, whom Linnell had befriended. A joint plaque on Old Wyldes now commemorates this friendship. Dickens was another distinguished lodger here in 1837, when recovering from the death of his sister-in-law, Mary Hogarth. The farmers had gone by 1884, when Charlotte Wilson lived here and started a revolutionary study circle called the Hampstead Historic Club. This was not concerned with local history, but with Fabian ideology, and Wyldes became a meeting place for Bernard Shaw, Sidney Webb, E Nesbit and other radical thinkers. The house was nearly razed to form a car park in 1905, when the Northern Line was dug underneath. A station was built here (under Hampstead Way) but never used. In 1906, the whole property was taken over by the Hampstead Garden Suburb Trust, partly as its estate office and partly as the home of its chief architect, Sir Raymond Unwin. A plaque on Wyldes notes his residence here 1906–40, but the family continued to occupy the house until 1967, when it was sold and divided up.

Return now up North End Way to Heath House and this time turn left into

SPANIARDS ROAD, which leads to another of Hampstead's border settlements. The ancient road, which is first named by the 1866 Ordnance Survey, is now higher than the surrounding Heath because of extensive sand quarrying on either side. In 1866–67, for instance, a quarter of an acre of sand and ballast was sold by the Lord of the Manor to the Midland Railway. Much sand was also removed for filling sandbags in two world wars. The street name derives from its climax, **The Spaniards Inn**, which is technically in the borough of Barnet, as the **boundary stones** show. (The 1799 stone marked FP means Finchley Parish, now part of Barnet.) Tradition has it that Spain's ambassador to the court of James I had a house on this site, and that his valet later started an inn. More likely, the name derives from the Spanish licensee registered in 1721. Here was also the lodge house and toll-gate for the Bishop of London's park, which stretched to the top of Highgate Hill (site of another toll-gate): the colony was then known as Parkgate. The 18th-century **toll-house**, which happily still slows down the traffic, was rescued by local conservationists (the Hampstead Heath and Old Hampstead Protection Society again) in 1967: its restoration reaped a Civic Trust Award. The present pub building dates from the

early 18th century, when the Spa brought rich custom for the tavern and its pleasure gardens.

In the Gordon Riots of 1780, Kenwood House, then occupied by the Earl of Mansfield, was saved from destruction – unlike his town house – when the landlord of the Spaniards offered the rioters unlimited refreshment at the inn. This delayed them sufficiently until the military, already alerted by the Mansfield family, arrived. The inn was popular with Dickens, who portrayed it in *The Pickwick Papers* and, some say, with Dick Turpin, not to mention Black Bess. (Some even remember the highwayman's very own pistol being fired nightly as a closing-time signal.)

Straddling the borough borders, and therefore liable to two separate rate demands, is **Erskine House**, adapted from the wing of an old house of that name which was demolished in 1923. The original 18th-century house was the home in the 1760s of John Sanderson, architect of the parish church, and from 1788 of Lord Erskine. This forensic genius, who even won the riotous Lord George Gordon's acquittal, with Lord Mansfield in the seat of judgement, expanded his garden across the road by building a tunnel. Erskine, who lived here until 1821, called his property **Evergreen Hill**, which is now the name of the house next door. To add to the confusion, this was once part of the adjoining **Heath End House**, which dates from about 1788. The latter was the home of the arctic explorer, Sir William Parry (1790-1855), who brought a pair of whale jaws here for a garden arch, and from 1889 of Canon and Mrs Barnett: she is better known as Dame Henrietta Barnett, prime promoter of Hampstead Garden Suburb. Now commemorated by a blue plaque, the Barnetts renamed the house St Jude's Cottage, after his Whitechapel parish, and turned old Erskine House into a convalescent home. In 1895 they lent their cottage to the American painter James McNeill Whistler, whose wife died here. The successful novelist Sir Hall Caine converted all this property to his liking in 1923, and stayed here until his death in 1931.

At the entrance to **SPANIARDS END**, a large mansion called The Firs was divided in the 1950s into **The White House** and **The Chantry**, with an unexpected extra called **Casa Maria**. The latter was adapted from the billiard room of The Firs and in a Spanish style, as this seemed appropriate to the area. The main house was built in 1734 by John Turner, a rich merchant (Park says tobacconist) of Fleet Street, who is credited with building the sandy road from here to North End, which still exists. Not so long-lived was the clump

of firs he planted hear his house, but at least these were frequently recorded by artists, including Constable. All the desirable 18th-century **cottages** in Spaniards End, which then descends into Barnet, were converted from the stables and garden sheds of The Firs.

On the other side of Spaniards Road are the fortress-like **Mount Tyndal** (1972) and another recent luxury development called **Spaniards Park**, which claims to be in Columbus Drive. Further west in several acres of grounds is a mansion still known as **The Elms**, but which functioned for some years as St Columba's Hospital. The property was sold to a sheikh in 1981 for over £2¹/₂ million pounds and resold a few years later for about £7 million. The house, built about 1875, is on the historic site of Mother Huff's Tea Gardens, which flourished here for 50 years from 1678. The art dealer Sir Joseph Joel Duveen, who added the Duveen Gallery to the British Museum and the Turner Wing to the Tate Gallery, lived at The Elms 1894–1908.

To the south of The Elms, but approachable only via East Heath Road, is the beautiful Heath-bound colony of **THE VALE OF HEALTH.** Traditionally, this was a place of refuge for 17th-century citizens fleeing the Great Plague of London. But tradition can be an ass. The name is not found

anywhere until 1801, and at the time of the plague this area was an unhealthy swamp. It was not until 1777 that the vale was drained by the Hampstead Water Company, which built the **pond** as a new reservoir. (The other Hampstead ponds were made in Tudor times.) The area was then known as Hatch's Bottom, as it was owned by Samuel Hatch, who also had property at the top of the hill. It seems likely that the Water Company re-christened the area thinking that their customers would not want their water from a place with such an insanitary name.

To the north of the pond is a small **fairground**, currently occupied by immobile homes. The ground has long been owned by the Gray family, who also ran the Vale of Health Hotel. This towering tavern, on the site of **Spencer House** (architect: L J Michaels), was built in 1863 (Fig 29), but was not a success. Parts were let out as factory, shops, Salvation Army barracks and studios. The artist Henry Lamb worked here from 1912–24: his portrait of Lytton Strachey, with a vaguely Vale background, is in the Tate. Stanley Spencer, after whom the flats are named, was here from 1924–27, mostly painting his *Cookham Resurrection*. The studio windows had to be removed to get the picture out (it is also in the Tate), as it was too big to take down the stairs.

To the west is **No.1 Byron Villas**, where a blue plaque salutes a brief appearance by D H Lawrence in 1915. This was the only London home that he and Frieda had: she came in order to be near the children of her first marriage, and he to see publication of *The Rainbow*. The novel caused outrage and was banned, and this, together with a Zeppelin raid they viewed from the Heath (described in his *Kangaroo*), hurried their departure to Cornwall. In the few months they were here, though, they held court in the Vale, with courtiers including Bertrand Russell, Aldous Huxley and Ottoline Morrell. Byron Villas were built in 1905 to replace a second Vale of Health Hotel from the 1860s, which also had a chequered career. Next door, the **Athenaeum** flats were built about 1960, on the site of an odd, chapel-like building, which at times housed an Anglo-German drinking club and at others the Salvation Army. Beyond the mini-spinney outside these flats is a **noticeboard** with a useful map of the Vale. There are no street names in the colony, and the GLC's attempts in 1966 to introduce names associated with

Constable were rebuffed by the residents.

Behind here, **Manor Lodge** is one of the Vale's oldest sizeable houses, basically early-18th-century. In the 1970s **Faircroft** was the home of theatre luminaries Trevor Nunn and Janet Suzman. Actor Alan Bates lived for many years at **Lavender Cottage**. To the south is **Hollycroft**, with a blue plaque to the social historians J L and

Barbara Hammond, who lived here from 1906–13. This was also the home from 1931 of Norman Bentwich, professor of international law, and of his wife Helen, one-time chairman of the LCC and author of the only history of the Vale of Health, first published in 1968.

Back north, another blue plaque on **Villas on the Heath** (not to be confused with Heath Villas) records the brief

29 The Hampstead Heath Hotel built in the Vale of Health in 1863 (lithograph by F Waller).

residence at **No.3** in 1912 of (Sir) Rabindranath Tagore. The following year, this Indian poet and mystic received the Nobel Prize for Literature, the first Asian to do so, and in 1915 he was knighted. This last honour he resigned 4 years later in protest against British policy in the Punjab. Nos.3–6 of this block are commended by Pevsner as 'attractive stuccoed Tudor of 1862'. To the east, the early-19th-century **Woodbine Cottage** was bought by Compton Mackenzie in 1937. He lived here off and on for 6 years, writing *The Four Winds of Love* and finding 'village life half an hour from Piccadilly Circus was a continuous refreshment and stimulus'.

All the houses to the north are early-19th-century, and most of them claim to have been the residence of the poet Leigh Hunt (see below). **Rose Cottage**, which is no exception, housed the impecunious Harmsworth family from 1870–73. The youthful Alfred and Harold, later to be press barons, were delighted to have George Jealous, editor of the *Ham&High*, as a near neighbour: he lived at **No.1 Villas on the Heath**. Jealous is said to have greatly inspired Alfred, the future Lord Northcliffe, with the gift of a toy printing set. It was another editor, Ernest Rhys of the Everyman Library, who changed the name to Hunt Cottage while living

there in the 1890s. Next door, **South Villa** has a home-made plaque to Leigh Hunt on its rear wall. **North Villa** may one day have a plaque to pianist Alfred Brendel, who lived here in the 1970s. **Vale Cottage** was Stella Gibbons' home in 1927–30. She wrote much of *Cold Comfort Farm* at her next Hampstead address, 67 Fitzjohn's Avenue. At the end of the road, **The Gables** are marked 1883 and have a healthy outlook, but John Middleton Murry (p 48), who lived at No.1a in the 1920s, was so ill that he called the area The Vale of Sickness.

Leigh Hunt came to the Vale of Health in 1815 and probably to **Vale Lodge**, at the north end of the hamlet. He wanted to recuperate from 2 years in gaol for slandering the Prince Regent, a deed which made him so popular that his time in prison was a triumph. But his fame followed him to the Vale and his literary circle increased. Keats first came to Hampstead to call on him here in 1816, and Shelley entertained his many children by sailing paper boats on the pond. The Hunt family finally left the Vale in 1921 and joined the migration of poets to Italy. Among much later inhabitants of Vale Lodge have been the thriller writer Edgar Wallace, Sir Leon Bagrit and Sir Paul Chambers, the latter two in the 1950s; both are mentioned elsewhere in this book. It

is worth exploring the narrow passage behind Vale Lodge to see the back of Rose Cottage and the picturesque, weather-boarded **Old Cottage**, listed as early-19th-century but looking much older. Up another alley to the west is **Chestnut Cottage**, dated about 1812 and for long the home of chimney sweeps.

Much has changed in the Vale of Health in its two centuries of development but, as in the rest of the surrounding area, much remains to surprise and delight the resident or visitor who wanders the streets of Hampstead.

Sources

Baines, F E. *Records of the manor, parish and borough of Hampstead.* Whitaker/Hewetson, 1890

Barratt, Thomas J. *The annals of Hampstead.* Black, 1912; Lionel Leventhal, 1972

Bebbington, Gillian. *London street names.* Batsford, 1977

Bentwich, Helen. *The Vale of Health.* High Hill Press, 1968; Camden History Society, 1977

Cherry, Bridget and Pevsner, Nikolaus. *The buildings of England – London 4: North.* Penguin, 1998

Hill, Mary. *Hampstead in light and shade.* Baines & Scarsbrook, 1938, 1945

Howitt, W. *The Northern Heights.* Longmans, 1869

Ikin, C W. *Hampstead Heath.* GLC, 1971

Kennedy, J. *The Manor and parish church of Hampstead.* Mayle, 1906

Maxwell, Anna. *Hampstead: its historic houses, its literary and artistic associations* James Clarke & Co., 1912

Norrie, Mavis and Ian (ed.). *The book of Hampstead.* High Hill Press, 1968

Oppé, E F. *Hampstead – a London town.* Author, 1951

Park, J J. *The topography and natural history of Hampstead.* Nichols, Son and Bentley, 1814, 1818

Pevsner, Nikolaus. *The buildings of England – London except the Cities of London and Westminster.* Penguin, 1952

Potter, G W. *Hampstead Wells.* Bell, 1904; Carlile House, 1978

Potter, G W. *Random recollections of Hampstead.* Eyre & Spottiswoode, 1907

Richardson, John. *Hampstead One Thousand (AD 986–1986).* Historical Publications 1985.

Thompson, F M L. *Hampstead, building a borough 1650–1964.* Routledge & Kegan Paul, 1974

Wade, Christopher. *For the poor of Hampstead, for ever.* Camden History Society, 1998

Walford, Edward. *Old and new London, vol. V.* Cassell, c.1880

White, Caroline A. *Sweet Hampstead and its associations.* Elliott, Stock 1900, 1903

The Hampstead Annuals 1897–1906. Mayle.

Maps

1746	Rocque	1864	Daw
1762	Ellis	1866	OS
1803	Goodwin	1891	Lowe
1814	Newton	1895	O.S.
1835	Cruchley	1915	O.S.
1847	Lee	1934	O.S.
1862	Weller	1953	O.S.

Other sources

Who's Who and *Who Was Who* (Black)

Dictionary of National Biography (OUP)

Hampstead and Highgate Express (Ham&High) (from 1872)

Camden Local Studies and Archives Centre, Holborn Library

Camden History Review Nos.1–23

52nd and 53rd List of Buildings of Special Architectural or Historic Interest (DOE 1974; DCMS 1998)

Blue Plaques on Houses of Historic Interest (GLC 1976, with additions)

LCC Street Lists and GLC Street Naming Section

Exhibition Catalogues of Hampstead Artists' Council

Victoria County History of Middlesex, vol IX (Hampstead and Paddington). OUP 1989

Index

Streets included in the survey are indicated in boldface, as are the main entries for these and other selected subjects;
* = illustration.